WOBURN

WOBURN

HIDDEN TALES OF A TANNERY TOWN

Marie Coady

THE
History
PRESS

Published by The History Press
Charleston, SC 29403
www.historypress.net

First published 2008

Manufactured in the United States

ISBN 978.1.59629.514.8

Library of Congress Cataloging-in-Publication Data
Coady, Marie.
Woburn : hidden tales of a tannery town / Marie Coady
p. cm.
ISBN 978-1-59629-514-8
1. Woburn (Mass.)--History--Anecdotes 2. Woburn (Mass.)--Social life and
customs--Anecdotes 3. Tanneries--Massachusetts--Woburn--History--Anecdotes 4.
Historic sites--Massachusetts--Woburn--Anecdotes 5. Woburn (Mass.)--Biography--
Anecdotes 6. Coady, Marie. I. Title.
F74.W89C63 2008
974.4'4--dc22
2008027632

Notice: The information in this book is true and complete to the best of our knowledge.
It is offered without guarantee on the part of the author or The History Press. The
author and The History Press disclaim all liability in connection with the use of this
book.

CONTENTS

CONTENTS

PREFACE

If you were not born and raised in the city of Woburn, the natives good-naturedly label you a Carpetbagger, and that's pretty much what I am. Although, in the spirit of reconciliation, one of Woburn's more progressive mayors presented me with a "proclamation" announcing that "the governing body of the City of Woburn has been petitioned to elevate Marie Coady to the august status of native Woburnite, thereby eliminating her previous lower rank as Carpetbagger." So, as an official Woburnite, I was then allowed to set forth to catalog the hidden stories in Woburn's history.

Actually, my interest in Woburn history was spurred on long before I became an official Woburnite. Having been born and raised in a house along the red line of the Freedom Trail and in the shadow of the Bunker Hill Monument in the Charlestown section of Boston, I couldn't help but be interested in the history that surrounded me.

Then, in 1993, while researching the Revolutionary soldier whose gravestone lay under my bedroom window in Charlestown, I found a Woburn connection. That's when I realized that Woburn is the quintessential community with six degrees of separation to people and places all over the world. Moreover, all of the stories I've uncovered prove beyond the shadow of a doubt that history does indeed repeat itself.

The opening chapters cover the uniqueness of the name that the founders chose for the then town of Woburn in 1642, and the subsequent chapters follow that uniqueness into the present day.

Because Woburn has two very historic and well-cared-for burial grounds, aptly enough named the First Burial Ground and the Second

Burial Ground, and when I leaned that it had been almost 150 years since an inventory of both burial grounds had been done, I decided to take on the challenge. With the encouragement of a friend in Winston, Georgia, who had strong ancestral connections to Woburn, I formed what became known as the Grave Group. With cameras in hand, the Grave Group set out to do a pictorial inventory of both burial grounds. All of our work was then posted on Toni Lasseter's Ye Olde Woburn website (http://www.yeoldewoburn.net).

Since roaming through graveyards oftentimes unearths skeletons, the Grave Group managed to uncover some of the really unique stories that I have catalogued in the subsequent chapters. That experience got me hooked and I kept looking in other places for skeletons in Woburn's closet, and found many. One of the most interesting stories I uncovered was Woburn's connection to the Boston Massacre, which I detail in a chapter of that title.

Because Woburn is a next-door neighbor to the town of Lexington, where the Battles of Lexington and Concord took place, Woburn's part in that battle often gets short shrift. With that in mind, I relate some of the events that mark Woburn's part in that famous battle in a chapter entitled "Restoring Battle Road's Human History." I would be remiss if I wrote anything about Woburn without at least mentioning its most illustrious family, the Baldwins. Toward that end, I catalogue the connection between Loammi Baldwin II and the Bunker Hill Monument.

Being a longtime member of the Woburn Historical Commission and being tasked with protecting Woburn's historic homes and landmarks has given me an opportunity to research the history of many historic houses in the city. One of the most unique and well-cared-for of those houses is the 1790 House. It was through my research into the social history of that elegant house that I came to know Eunice Carter Thompson, and I share her story in a chapter entitled "Born in the 1970 House." I think you will find it compelling.

There are also the tragic stories of murder and mayhem as well as the loss of five members of the same family to the deep, dark waters of Woburn's Horn Pond. Woburn also has its urban legends and I reveal one of the more interesting ones here for you to enjoy. Other chapters cover the darker stories that have left a legacy of Superfund sites and wells that poisoned many children. It's a battle that continues to this day.

Then there are the stories that inspire, one of which is entitled "Walnut Hill and the Great Depression, circa 1936." This story tells how a community came together to save a desperately poor widow from abject poverty during the Depression. Another story, "Woburn's Ya-Ya Sisterhood," will fill you with delight as it tells of a lifetime of friendships that not only stood the test of time but distance. There are also the stories that prove that the more things change the more they stay the same, including "Same-Sex Marriage, circa 1878"; "Suicidal Parrots and Gypsy Royalty"; "Woburn's Ovaltine Connection"; and "If Walls Could Talk."

Most of the hidden stories I tell in this book were uncovered by poring through old newspapers, and my research disproves the old saying that yesterday's newspaper is only good for lining the birdcage. That's where the hidden history of a community can be found, reincarnated and enhanced by implementing today's research tools.

I would be remiss if I didn't mention the many people who helped in making this book come alive, namely the people who shared their photo collections and skills toward that end. A special thanks to fellow historians John McElhiney and Tom Smith for sharing their wonderful historic photos from their very unique collections, and also to Bud Fowle for sharing photos from his family's collection. Since I am a writer and not a photographer, my very special gratitude goes to Gerry Kehoe of Innitou Photo for sharing her photographic skills. Gerry made special trips to the First and Second Burial Grounds to capture the unique inscriptions on gravestones there that tell the most interesting stories. Many of the other photos were shared with me by the people who also shared their family stories and they are duly noted in the image credits.

As my proclamation declaring me no longer a Carpetbagger concluded: "Marie Coady shall be known to all natives of North, South, East and West Woburn, as well as Mount Misery, Central Square and Rag Rock as NATIVE WOBURN CITIZEN MARIE COADY, thereby eliminating all her whining about her previous Carpetbagger status." And for that I am grateful. I am also grateful to Mayor Robert Dever for making me feel at home here in Woburn and for helping me to stop "whining."

WOBURN, WOOBOURNE, WOODBURN OR WHATEVER

What's in a name? That which we call a rose by any other name would smell as sweet.
– Shakespeare, Romeo and Juliet

When the Pilgrims first arrived on the shores of the Massachusetts Bay Colony, their aim was to settle as much of King Charles's land grant as they could. Part of that process was choosing names for each settlement and, as would be expected, they chose names that reminded them of home. For instance, Boston is named for a town in Lincolnshire, England, the hometown of one of those first settlers. Then, as the settlers fanned out to settle more of the Charlestown Grant, they followed that same rule. The problem was that many of the names they chose morphed over time into words that were difficult to pronounce, and the city of Woburn is a perfect example of that problem.

In spite of the fact that Wooborne, Wooburn, Woobun, Woeburn, Wohbun, Woobahn, Wuhbun and Oburn still lead Woburnites home, pronunciation is still a problem. And whether Woburn is your adopted city, the home of your ancestors or the home you chose because it was conveniently located between Routes 93 and 128 and the taxes were low, Woburn is now home to some thirty-five thousand residents, most of whom can't agree on the pronunciation of their hometown's name.

What is the correct pronunciation? Well, even if the correct pronunciation can finally be determined, one cannot blame anyone for mispronouncing it, because like Haverhill, Leicester and Worcester, Woburn is one of those names chosen at random by English settlers that came to defy the rules of American phonics. And to make matters worse, people from other parts of

Quarter-Millennial Arch looking northeast on Main Street from the Unitarian Church in 1892. *Courtesy of John McElhiney.*

the country have no yardstick to measure its pronunciation by. All of this begs the question: Who would do such a thing?

One theory was proposed by Woburn's Samuel Sewell, well known for his *History of Woburn*. Sewell claims that the name Woburn was chosen "in honor of the Hon. Richard Russell" who came to Charlestown in 1640 from Hertfordshire, England, and was a relative of the Russell family in Bedfordshire, England, which was located in Woburn, England. Sewell's contention was backed up by the fact that the Russell estate was actually named "Woburn Abbey." If that's not confusing enough, he added that when Charlestown Village (i.e., Woburn) was incorporated in 1642 and needed a name, Captain Robert Sedgwick, along with two other deputies of the general court, picked the name Woburn because of their high regard for the Honorable Richard Russell.

To add to the confusion, Sedgwick wasn't actually on site when the town's name was chosen because there was some sort of falling out and he "abandoned the struggling babe" of a town before it was named. But to be fair, he was among the men who supplied the money for the expedition and settlement of the town. So, in their infinite wisdom, instead of naming the town Sedgwick, they named it after the town where Sedgwick was

The 250th Anniversary Arch commemorating the founding of Wooborne, formerly Charlestowne Village, 1892. *Courtesy of John McElhiney.*

baptized, namely Woburn, Bedfordshire, England, and where the esteemed Richard Russell had relatives. To further complicate matters, those intrepid seven men who took on the wilderness between Routes 93 and 128 spelled it *Wooborne*, the pronunciation of which remains today, in spite of its spelling being changed to *Woburn* sometime later on.

Today, a search of a United States atlas and a Web search of MapQuest turns up only two other spots in the United States called Woburn. When I refer to them as spots, I mean just that. They are not cities, towns or even villages.

Woburn, Illinois, is located in the southwestern part of Illinois some distance, as the crow flies, off of Route 140, near the town of Greenville and equidistant from Vandalia, which is smack dab at the intersection of Routes I-70 and 40. Woburn, Illinois, could be a beautiful spot, as it is near the shores of Governor Bond Lake; unfortunately, the people I talked to in Greenville and Vandalia had no idea where or what Woburn is. In fact, when I called 411 for information, there was no listing for anything called Woburn in Illinois. The operator was apologetic and somewhat perplexed by my request for a listing, any listing, in Woburn, Illinois.

The North Dakota long-distance operator was perplexed as well when I requested a listing for Woburn, North Dakota. It seems that this Woburn is so close to the Saskatchewan border that you could throw a rock at it, and the nearby towns of Bowbells, Lignite and Couteau have no idea where Woburn is either. Once again, our sister city in North Dakota is set in the middle of nowhere and lies unrecognized by most. But I'm still hopeful of finding someone in the area who may recognize Woburn, North Dakota, or Woburn, Illinois, and know their histories.

But Woburn, Quebec, in Canada is thriving. They even have hotels, motels, bed-and-breakfasts and a few restaurants. It is the quintessential bedroom community, lying close to the borders of Maine and Vermont but retaining a unique French flavor. But Woburn, Quebec, is the only other spot in North America named Woburn that retains a clear sense of its history. In fact, in its Treasure Gallery museum, it displays a diorama created by a hometown boy, Archelus Poulin, who is said to have been an important folk artist in Canada between 1892 and 1969. Poulin's diorama vividly depicts three aspects of rural life in Quebec and is entitled, appropriately enough, "Ploughing Time, Seeding Time, Fence Time."

When I contacted the Hotel Motel Arnold in Woburn, Quebec, I was greeted with "bonjour" and some other phrase I never mastered in my three years of high school French. When I said, "Parlez vous Anglais?" the young girl on the other end seemed mortified and apologized profusely. At least I think she did. In any case, she put someone on the line who spoke some Anglais.

I introduced myself as a fellow Woburnite from Massachusetts and the gentleman warmed to my request, which was simply, "How do you pronounce 'Woburn' there?" His answer was much as I expected. He said clearly, "Woo-burn," but put a French spin on it that made it sound somehow sweeter than the manner it was pronounced in the movie *A Civil Action*, based in Woburn, Massachusetts.

Of course, our namesake city is Woburn, England, which has been referred to as our "mother town" and was a destination for Woburnites doing grand tours in the more genteel nineteenth century.

Woburn, England, has been the seat of the Duke of Bedfordshire for more than 350 years and lays claim to Woburn Abbey and the great Woburn Safari Park. Woburn Abbey is on three thousand acres of land and boasts a beautiful eighteenth-century mansion built by Cistercian monks in 1145 and "confiscated" (or, more plainly, stolen) by King Edward VI, who then granted it to John Russell in 1574. It is said to contain "one of the most private art collections in the world," which means, "Look but don't touch."

Thus we are stuck with a moniker that is mostly mispronounced and that you are more often than not asked to spell when ordering from the LL. Bean catalogue.

THE SOUTH END OF 1900

As the clock ticks toward a new millennium, the authentic voices of the twentieth century begin to fade into history. Soon the only resources left for us to experience those decades will be volumes of dusty and sometimes-dull history tomes, inanimate photos, selected films and tape recordings of occasions deemed worthy of note by the keepers of the archives.

I have no doubt there will be volumes of information readily available to the public about wars, presidents, assassinations, disasters and other national and world-shattering events that left indelible impressions on history. But who will capture and store the flavor, the sights, the sounds and the smells of a century of everyday life in a community like Woburn when all those who experienced it are gone?

Life in Woburn at the beginning of the twentieth century was very different from the Woburn of today with its paved roads, clean air, running water and indoor bathroom facilities. Areas of Woburn that were once farmland have been transformed into suburban neighborhoods and our population has swelled from twelve thousand in the late 1880s to more than thirty-five thousand today, and growing. Even the old neighborhoods, especially the South End, have evolved into more residential neighborhoods, a stark contrast to the industrial centers they were in the early 1900s. That was a time when tanneries dominated the landscape, and the houses that lined the streets, within only a few feet of those tanneries, belonged to tannery owners and were less than luxurious.

According to the memoirs of the late Dr. Thomas J. Glennon (entitled *Early Life*), the South End of Woburn was a world apart—a world so

Tannery in the backyards of workers' houses in the South End of Woburn, circa 1900. *Courtesy of the Linscott/Smith Collection.*

different from the experiences of other children growing up only a few miles away that it seemed like another planet.

Glennon describes his house in the South End about 1900 as

> *a tannery house, a wooden structure of two tenements…the rear wall of which stood no more than 20 feet from the liquor pits housed in a low flat-roofed building, dim windowed and bleak. A high fence afforded the only barrier between kitchen and the refuse from the vats which was dumped in the intervening space. The result was a large pool of brown liquor, soft and slimy at first, but soon becoming solid…with winter's low temperatures and forming the neighborhood's dirty ice rink.*

What Glennon remembers most is dirt. Dirt roads and yards turned to a muddy quagmire after a downpour. He remembers that mud oozing through his toes on warm days—most children in his neighborhood had no shoes in summer. He also remembers the bucket of water that always stood at the backdoor in which he'd wash the mud off before entering the kitchen; in winter months he'd get a taste of the strap for not removing his muddy shoes before tramping across his mother's recently washed kitchen floor.

The bare wooden frame house where Glennon lived on John Street had few of life's amenities. "The kitchen furnishings," he explains, "were minimal in number and efficiency—a black coal stove, a shallow iron sink with one cold water faucet, a bare table with few wooden chairs, a rough board floor and a kerosene bracket lamp set in a frame on the wall."

Glennon remembers his mother "blackening" the kitchen stove faithfully once a week with stove black, an oily substance that made the stove shine an ebony color that passed for clean yet removed the soot accumulated from a week of burning the soft coal, which produced so much soot that it seemed to be everywhere. The floor she guarded so diligently against the onslaught of muddy shoes was swept daily and scrubbed once a week with a scrubbing brush as she went down on all fours and dragged a pail of water alongside her. But that bare wooden floor took its toll on his mother's knees, and Glennon describes them as "splinter-laden."

Upstairs were two bare bedrooms with iron beds and an old-fashioned commode in the corner of each room so you wouldn't have to stumble to the outhouse in the dark of night. No heat and no rugs meant your feet were greeted every morning by cold, bare floors—guaranteed to wake you with a start. Since the only source of heat in the house was that old iron stove in the kitchen, he remembers that during a cold snap, bedroom windows were covered with ice for days at a time.

Main Street, before it was paved in 1917, with the Dow Block at the center. *Courtesy of John McElhiney.*

Inside Linnell's Market as it looked in January 1913. *Left to right*: employees Gerald Turner, Frank Turner, Fred Turner and owner James H. Linnell. *Courtesy of John McElhiney.*

There were even periods when that kitchen stove would be stone-cold for lack of that sooty, soft coal. Those were what tannery workers called the "slack periods." During those periods, there was no money for coal and young Glennon helped out by "coke picking" through a pile of cinders at the gasworks nearby.

At age eight, Glennon discovered that if he rose before 6:00 a.m. and made his way to the pile of discarded cinders, he could pick through the waste and find pieces big enough to support a flame, and he was not alone on those cold mornings. Other children, younger than he, were regulars at the gasworks. Glennon also found he could pick nearly a bushel of coal before school. He would continue this chore throughout the summer months so he could lay in an ample supply of coal to boil the water for the tea that they drank three times a day, and bake the large loaves of bread that made up their diet. Milk and sugar was considered a luxury, but the hot tea warmed them through the winter months and the bread, as simple as it was, filled hungry bellies.

The tanneries played a large part in everyone's life. It was the father's place of employment and the bane of the mother's existence as she fought the soot that settled on her newly washed clothes, but it also provided an interesting place for children of the South End to wile away the hours exploring the nine tanneries that lined the railroad tracks between Green and Cross Streets. There were also freight cars in which impish young boys could elude the cop on the beat, and the gasworks and iron foundry offered perfect places for curious young boys to explore as well.

Glennon continues: "Along the spur tracks between freight cars and buildings there was a narrow space, out of sight of passersby and far enough removed from houses to allow exaggerated and loud common talk to those who drink more than is necessary for mild stimulation." That meant there were lots of bottles to collect and sell to the local liquor dealer and make a tidy profit. But sometimes, he said, "it hurt to find the bottles smashed on the rail or against the cars." He saw that as wasteful and denying his family some revenue.

One tannery house Glennon lived in belonged to the Murdock Tannery and his kitchen window was "no more than twenty feet from the dankest and most odiferous of all the ramifications of a sprawling tannery, the liquor pit building," and he describes that building perfectly:

Beyond the liquor pits loomed the five-storied red shop, or tannery with its steeply pitched roof and two small smokestacks. These last belched forth constantly huge volumes of black smoke, the waste from soft burning coal. Soot spread over the neighborhood, befouling the clothes, newly washed and strung on a line which stretched from the fence to a hook near the kitchen door. In open fields nearby, newly tanned half hides, brown and wet, were draped on racks for drying, exuding the characteristic, obnoxious tannery odor.

But beyond the odiferous odor of tanneries, Glennon also remembers the corner store and its smell of sour pickles, crackers, bread and kerosene. He would watch in amazement as the "store lady," the widow Annie Ahern (herself the mother of two boys and two girls), disappeared behind a "maze of boxes and barrels" and returned with a "bag of flour, rolls of fly paper and even a broom or washboard." His ambition as a young boy was to work at the candy counter in widow Ahern's store. He could think of no better profession than to oversee the broad flat cases that held the trays of candy that sold for three or four pieces for a penny.

He also remembers the smell and sights of the corner meat market, the faces of friends and the sights and sounds of the pushcart men shouting out for junk, bottles, rags and bones, the stuff of their livelihood. He remembers the sound of an occasional automobile that would invade the neighborhood, causing everyone to stare at the strange sight, as well as the buggies and wagons that were more frequent vehicles along the unpaved streets of the South End. On dry, dusty days they'd work up a mean cloud of dust, and in wet weather would spray mud on your clothes as they passed by.

Dr. Thomas J. Glennon has left a treasury of memories in his thirty-eight-page documented history of his "early life," but his greatest contribution is that through his vibrant words he has been able to recapture the smells of every facet of his neighborhood, the feel of the cold as his feet hit the floor each winter morning and the warm mud oozing through his toes in summer. He also captures the sight of a sky filled with soot raining down on a neighborhood that no longer remembers what it used to be.

Woburn "Road Report," 2000

I had a friend who loved to drive through Woburn Center. She said it brought back memories—both good and bad. But when she found out she had only a few months to live, it became a great source of comfort for her to have me drive her slowly down Main Street as she reminisced along the way. Sometimes I'd leave my mini-tape on and record her voice as it waxed and waned between delight and pathos, melodrama and unbridled laughter.

When her illness finally took its toll and left her housebound and bedridden, she would listen to those tapes over and over, reliving her trips down Main Street and along Memory Lane. It gave her untold comfort.

Author Thomas Wolfe once said, "You can't go home again." But for those threatened with extinction or overcome with a sentimental longing brought on by age, home is the only place that will do. For it is home that holds the origins of their memories and the subsequent comfort they provide. And for those who grew up in this city when Woburn Center was in its heyday, nostalgia colors their view of the bricks and mortar that form the backdrop for lives lived and memories stored in dreams of what used to be.

But did you ever wonder what strangers see, with no nostalgia to blur their vision, as they travel through Woburn Center and along Main Street for the first time?

Well, a few years ago, on a perfect summer evening, a stranger came to town. His name was Z, and he slipped quietly down Main Street on the evening of June 17 and blended in so neatly that no one guessed he wasn't a Woburnite.

Z was traveling cross-country, and like Jack Kerouac or Charles Kurault, Z was on the road in search of America. Little is known about Z. I came across him quite by accident on the Internet. But one thing is sure. He is thoughtful and observant and not only saw Woburn Center for the first time in June of 1998, he wrote about it, too.

Fortunately, although his words flashed across the screen in what now seems a wink in time, it was long enough for me to capture Z's "Road Report," delivered to his friends and family as he laid bare a pristine view of Woburn Center for us to ponder, for good or ill.

It seems Z had gotten as far as Woburn toward the end of a long day on the road and decided he couldn't stand one more minute sitting in his car. He arrived on an otherwise ordinary Wednesday and registered as a guest at a hotel just off Route 93, shed his auto and then began walking down Montvale Avenue toward Woburn Center.

When he neared the end of Montvale and saw Woburn Center just ahead, he readied his poetic eye and sharp intuition, mentally recording what he saw and heard. Then, sitting in Woburn House of Pizza with a plate of Chicken al Greco in front of him, he flashed his road report across the World Wide Web for everyone to read.

His words grabbed me, and although I didn't know why at the time, I quickly hit print and captured them for future reference. And it's a good thing, too, because a recent Web search proved fruitless—I discovered that Z's "Road Report," chronicling his short stay in "Woburn ("Woobahn"), Mass.," had slipped into that black chasm of "Data Missing."

You may not like everything Z had to say about our city, which he, as most do, referred to as a town. But through his prose we may come to gain valuable insight into the way things really are from someone who had no vested interest in Woburn's redevelopment, or the lack of it, when he chronicled his first impressions of Woburn Center.

Z's "Road Report" reads as follows:

> *Woburn ("Woobahn"), Mass.—Couldn't stand to spend another moment in the car and decided to walk into town and find a restaurant for dinner. The restaurant pickings are slim but—What a town! Finally found my way into the "Woburn House" where they have surf-n-turf on the menu. Ordered "Chicken al Grecco."*
>
> *Woburn is a total New England town—very working class, very industrial, on the skids, living in hopeful unease with the post-industrial sprawl just beyond its borders. The streets are full of hot rods and huge*

A 1968 view of the Woburn Common as it looked before the hill behind the storefronts on Main Street was removed for the present parking lot. *Courtesy of the Linscott/Smith Collection.*

motorcycles. The gas station in the middle of town has a big old copper dome on top and sez "Theirs is good, ours is BEST" around the base.

The center of town is ABSOLUTELY GORGEOUS! Buildings ranging in age from the Edwardian Era all the way back to some that are severe enough to be pre-Revolutionary. Curiously, they had all been converted to multi-occupant commercial zoning and are occupied by dentists, photography studios and law offices. Why is it that in these latter years, buildings that used to comfortably enclose a single family farm are now economically viable only as micro-business parks?

No one who has never lived through a New England spring can possibly know how soft and sweet the air is this evening. The temperature is such that when air moves over your skin it feels deliciously cool and when it stands still it feels balmy—and it is supersaturated with scents: flowers, fruit, rust, new-mown grass, rotting vegetable matter, exhaust fumes and...rust.

Passed two beauty shops with (guess what...) Patrick Nagel prints in the windows and two music stores with posters of big-hair metal guys.

Women in the next booth talking about astrology. Ultra-Italian guy in a backwards gimme hat explaining computers to his (very quiet) date in the booth in front of me. He probably plays heavy metal, and she probably wants to quit her job and move to NYC.

Chicken al Grecco is a lot of food. Still working on it.

Hope all is well, Z

25

Maybe Z didn't get it all right, but when he dubbed Woburn "working class," we all know he showed great insight. And when he added that Woburn was "on the skids," he pinpointed the one first impression we can work at changing.

So when the Woburn Downtown Revitalization Committee begins to implement their plans to change a newcomer's first impression from "on the skids" to "ABSOLUTELY BEAUTIFUL," don't think only of your memories, but of the memories we can create for the next generation.

A Ghastly, Ghostly Task Joyously Performed

C emeteries are much more than repositories for the dead. They contain the essence of our collective and individual life, and are the repositories of a community's most cherished values.

The First Burial Ground is one such link to the past, and if you can find it tucked away behind the hustle and bustle of Main Street, or perched precariously atop one of the few hills Woburn Center hasn't tamed, you can stroll it's helter-skelter lanes and stoop from time to time to read inscriptions, worn by time, that reveal the virtues and foibles of our humanity.

Hence it was that a grave group (officially known as the Grave Group, made up of Woburn Chat listserv friends) gathered over the gravestones at the First Burial Ground on Park Street in Woburn one pleasant Saturday to deliberate the genesis of a grainy, sandstone memorial carelessly cast off and resting haphazardly on the ground. As the gathering continued to gaze at the reddish, brick-kilned slab, with indentations both rotund and rectangular, each had their own guess as to what it was and how it came to be discarded and dispossessed.

I guessed it was the covering for an ancient well, while another offered it may have been a trough or watering place for horses when horses were the main mode of transportation. Yet another suggested it may have been a cistern, whatever that is, but it certainly sounded erudite, and I am not one to argue with the seemingly informed.

Then, a more observant member of the group spied four granite footings just next to it, jutting out of the ground like the legs of a tableless table. It was at this point that the discussion turned to speculation as to what might have been balanced on those sturdy granite legs, none of which—now that I know the truth—seems at all plausible. So it was that the grave group continued to congregate above the dearly departed to perform the ghoulish task of cataloguing the ghostly remains of the long-gone and garnering ghastly data to be recorded for future generations.

Judy Wood was our most enthusiastic gravestone recorder. She could call to mind verses carved on ancient gravestones her mother had introduced her to as a child. It was also Judy who suggested the Fitting Feast that took place when our work was done. But it was Judy's brother, Tony Cobb, who made the most important contribution when he sent via UPS a box of "Chocolates To Die For" from far off Ohio to top off our Fitting Feast.

Judy, ever encouraged by fellow digger of graves Nancy Spolidoro, suggested delectable delights such as gummy worms, Fowle sandwiches and "Cask of Amontillado" wine, while Nancy encouraged us all to sing "I've Got You Under My Skin," hum the theme song from "The Naked and the Dead" or recite "Tales from the Crypt" while afoot on the dearly departed's remains.

Doris McKee, ever the mother, clucked over us all and made sure we did not tire, go hungry or injure ourselves in our careless jaunt. It was also Doris who provided vampire wine and just about every comfort one could ask for to make a Fitting Feast fitting.

Rosie Runfolo, appropriately attired in a Devil's baseball cap and carrying Devil Dogs, manned a digital camera to record our every move, and many of the tombstones as well, for posterity.

Carol Johnson had her grandson, Joey Paris, in tow for the express purpose of visiting a direct descendant, Captain Edward Johnson, one of Woburn's early settlers and the author of *The Wonder-working Providence of Sion's Saviour in New England.*

Lamentably, the venerable captain and many of Woburn's early founders' original grave makers were fashioned of wood and had long since become food for the worms, as had they. Hence their graves appeared unmarked by the 1800s, and when the town confiscated the western section of the burial ground for an animal pound, they unearthed several skeletons and interred them in an unmarked, common grave somewhere on the present burial ground.

Nathaniel Saltonstall's grave site showing granite pillars carved by Nathan Lamson and the sandstone slab where steel plates had once been embedded. *Courtesy of Gerry Kehoe, Innitou Photo.*

Their burial site was later memorialized by an elegant marker erected in 1976 by the Woburn Minutemen in celebration of the bicentennial. Unfortunately, it was nowhere in sight when Captain Johnson's young descendant came to pay his respects, as it was at another location undergoing some necessary repairs.

Getting back to the carelessly discarded, reddish sandstone slab resting beside those granite table legs that appeared to have no purpose, allow me shed some light on that mystery.

It seems, on the evening of June 23, 1739, Nathaniel Saltonstall, Esq., died suddenly in Woburn. Since Nathaniel was recently "removed" to Woburn from Boston, it was determined he would be buried in Woburn's First Burial Ground.

Stranger still is that before Nathaniel departed this life, he had ordered large amounts of money to be disbursed to the following: Ebenezer Kendall to dig his grave; Isaac Snow to provide coffin plates made of lead and engraved with an inscription and his coat of arms (the lead plates were confiscated during the Revolution to make bullets); Nathan Lamson, stonecutter from Charlestown, to carve four granite pillars; and Thomas Moulin to kiln the massive sandstone slab and act as "pall and portage" to carry it to its resting place and balance it atop the four granite pillars.

Gravestone of Elizabeth Cotton that once lay atop Nathaniel Saltonstall's sandstone slab. Sometime later it was placed on the ground where it lays today. *Courtesy of Gerry Kehoe, Innitou Photo.*

Three years later, Elizabeth Cotton went mysteriously to her final reward, and sometime following her interment, the slate slab commemorating her death was found curiously resting atop Nathaniel's sandstone slab, obscuring the latter from view.

Even more curious is the fact that the inscription on Elizabeth's stone has been one of the major curiosities at the burial ground since its inception. But I'll let you judge for yourself. The inscription reads:

Here lyes the Remains of M'rs (Mistress) Elizabeth Cotton,
Daughter of the Rev'd Roland
Cotton late of Sandwich Dec'd; Who died a VIRGIN
October 12'th 1742, AEtais (age) 46.

If a Virgin Marry She hath not sinned. Nevertheless Such
shall have trouble in the Flesh. But He
that giveth her not in Marriage doth better. She
is happier if She so Abide.

To add another hint of mystery, it is important to note that Elizabeth Cotton was no stranger to Nathaniel Saltonstall. She was his niece.

Both Nathaniel Saltonstall's and Elizabeth Cotton's grave markers now rest on the ground, scattered carelessly, while the four granite pillars that once held them both aloft point to the sky with no real purpose.

WOBURN'S
CONNECTION TO THE
BOSTON MASSACRE

The Richardson name is as common as Smith or Jones in all fifty states. And since the three original progenitors of the prolific Richardson family line sowed the seeds for an unending line of descendants right here in Woburn, I was not surprised when one of those descendents contacted me to assist her in unearthing her Richardson roots.

Unfortunately, in the course of my research I uncovered a family skeleton of historic proportions and it was my duty to inform the Oregon branch of the Richardson family of my findings. Fortunately, they were delighted to have a skeleton that is mentioned in the same breath as the Boston Massacre.

That vile skeleton was one Ebenezer Richardson, great-great-grandson of Samuel Richardson, born March 31, 1718, the son of Timothy and Abigail (Johnson) Richardson. And as it turns out, there is not room enough in this chapter of Woburn's hidden history to tell everything I've discovered about Ebenezer Richardson. But just to give you an idea of how truly loathsome Ebenezer Richardson was, it helps to know that he was not only the father of widow Henshaw's child, he was also her brother-in-law. Yes, Ebenezer was married to Keziah Henshaw's sister, Rebecca Fowle Richardson. And there was no lack of raised eyebrows when Ebenezer married Rebecca soon after she was widowed by the death of her first husband, another Richardson, Lieutenant Phineas Richardson, in 1738. It seems many wondered why a young man of twenty-two would marry a woman twelve years his senior.

As stated in *The Richardson Memorial*, a lofty tome chronicling the genealogy of that prolific family: "That Ebenezer Richardson married

"Though hampered by indignities, Mr. Ebenezer Richardson fully embodied all of mankind's truly righteous traits which, along with his fabled singlemindedness of purpose, inspired what became my most memorable character. I am forever in Mr. Richardson's debt."
— Charles Dickens

Get out of my yard!

Get out of my sight!

And thus our noble stock again
Rose up to grasp the responsibility of men,
And rights and, indeed, recognition earned
Set a timely example for all those concerned.

Drawing by one of the Richardson descendants that appears in the updated version of the Richardson Family Genealogy. *Courtesy of Gina Richardson.*

this woman, though much older than himself, is rendered certain by a law suit" initiated by Rebecca's family sometime after her third child, Ebenezer, was born in 1746. The suit alleged that Ebenezer indeed had only married Rebecca for her money and property. This also gives a good indication as to what many thought of Ebenezer's character, even at the callow age of twenty-two. But for Ebenezer, the passage of time brought no learning curve. He just kept topping one dastardly act with another.

It does appear that Ebenezer attempted to make an honest woman of Keziah as an early entry in Boston's Vital Records indicates. On January

12, 1754, marriage intentions were posted in Boston between a Keziah Henshaw and Ebenezer Richardson, and the happy couple tied the knot on May 15, 1754, but they did not live happily after.

That entry also indicates that Ebenezer wisely left Woburn for Boston's North End as early as 1754, but it took him no time at all to build himself a similarly vile reputation there as one of the more aggressive customs officers (who were as beloved in Revolutionary times as today's IRS agents). By 1760, according to Hiller Zobel's book, *The Boston Massacre*, Ebenezer had earned himself the reputation as being "vile unmatched in Boston," and the title of "Informer." He even bragged that he "[g]ave good information of several breeches of the Acts of Trade and Seizure were made and the Vessels and Goods condemned." Well, you can imagine how popular his attitude made him with the local Sons of Liberty.

By 1767, things in Boston had heated up substantially and since Ebenezer's job was to provide the board of customs with a list of merchants who avoided paying the importation taxes forced on them by an act of English Parliament that year, you can imagine what a perfect target he was for the Sons of Liberty. Not only did he comply with the mandates of his new position, he went about it with gusto and was only too happy to provide the custom's office with lists of "merchants or others who imported or sold articles on which duties had been imposed." In fact, he was the most vocal of customs officials and "consequently he and his like were extremely obnoxious to the people."

So much was he reviled that even the young boys targeted him with sneers, jeers and an occasional pelting of mud and rotten fruit. There were so many instances of Ebenezer's "vile" reputation that there is not enough room in this column to enumerate them for you. But there is one instance that is too important to leave out.

On the morning of February 22, 1770, while Ebenezer was making his way to his home in the North End and neared the house of his "friend," neighbor and fellow customs official, Theophilus Lillie, he came upon a group of young street toughs who had erected a post outside his house "with a hand affixed pointing at (him) in derision," a device used by the radicals in the town to signify an informer.

Richardson took offense and tried to persuade a teamster to "drive his cart against the post and break it down." The teamster refused and a crowd gathered. Now the group of boys turned on Richardson and chased him to his house and began throwing "bricks and stones" at his windows. This only served to make the belligerent Ebenezer even

Boston Massacre, March 5, 1770. *Chromolithograph by John Bufford.*

angrier, and true to his character he made a bad situation worse by shouting threats at a mob that had now forgotten all about Theophilus Lillie and turned their anger on him.

But Richardson was now no longer alone. He was joined by a disgruntled sailor, George Wilmot, out of work because his ship, *Liberty*, had been burned out from under him by an angry mob in Rhode Island. At one point Richardson came out of the house and shook a stick at the crowd, promising to "make a lane" through them. That was the signal for the crowd to begin pelting the windows with bricks, smashing them as well as the frames around them until Richardson shouted that the "sticks, stones [and] eggs" had struck his wife Keziah and his two daughters.

At this point, Ebenezer lost it and went for his musket, aimed it out the window and pretended to shoot, but the gun wasn't loaded and clicked harmlessly. That gesture only served to make the crowd angrier, and they surrounded the house and began battering down the doors. This time, with his gun fully loaded, Ebenezer came purposefully to the window, "rested the barrel" on the windowsill and let loose a barrage of swan shot that took down Christopher Seider (or Sneider), "a poor German boy, eleven or twelve years old," and injured several others.

But even at that, Richardson wasn't through. Once again he aimed at the crowd and shouted, "Damn ye come here! I'm ready for you!" Even

The bloody massacre perpetrated on King Street in Boston on March 5, 1770.
Engraving by Paul Revere.

when a call went out for help and thousands arrived on the scene and grabbed the gun from him, Ebenezer would not give up. He ran for his cutlass and fended off the group, refusing to surrender until a "proper officer" arrived.

This act of violence, one upon the other, was the culmination of years of agitation by what Tory loyalists considered Whig "rabble." Only two weeks later, on March 5, 1770, the Boston Massacre "added to the general excitement and prepared the people for a forcible and bloody resistance." Hence began in earnest the Revolutionary War. Some historians attribute Ebenezer Richardson's actions as the catalyst for all that followed.

Unfortunately, Ebenezer never learned anything as a result of what some may consider a life-altering experience. Even his actions in court at his trial for the murder of Christopher Seider/Sneider did nothing to mellow a man filled with an anger no one could quell, and life kept giving him a pass.

Ebenezer was charged and found guilty of murder and spent a scant two years in prison before he received not only a pardon from the king but "an appointment as an officer of the customs in Philadelphia." It seems the king was grateful for Ebenezer's previous service as a snitch in Boston, turning in "merchants who imported or sold" goods and neglected to pay the tax. Upon release from jail, he left town in the dark of night, "for there was an intention to give him a coat of tar and feathers."

But one person, it appears, did finally turn over a new leaf. According to Boston records, a Keziah Richardson married a William Smith on December 29, 1776, and started the New Year of 1777 with a new name and a new husband. Whether that Keziah was Ebenezer's wife or daughter still needs to be discovered, but by acquiring the name Smith, it's a cinch that it offered some anonymity for one of Ebenezer's womenfolk.

THE GRAVE GROUP
REGROUPS

Fall was in the air and the turn of the second millennium loomed, so it seemed a fitting time to send out a call for the Grave Group to reorganize, this time at the Second Burial Ground on Montvale Avenue, and for three successive Saturdays they recorded and photographed each gravestone in the Second Burial Ground.

But what could it be that would compel a group of otherwise ordinary mortals to undertake such a ghoulish task? The answer comes from a distance. It wafts across the Internet from Winston, Georgia, and through the sheer force of tenacious commitment, manifests itself in the person of one Toni Lasseter.

My first contact with Toni came through her website dedicated to the city of Woburn, its people and its history. You see, Toni Lasseter is the sole force behind the award-winning Ye Olde Woburn Website, launched on November 5, 1998, a storehouse of Woburn's past and available to anyone with an Internet connection. When Toni decided to add an inventory, with pictures, of Woburn's First and Second Burial Grounds to her website, the Grave Group responded, because what Toni wants Toni gets.

But why, you might ask, would a woman from Georgia be interested in cataloguing Woburn's history? The answer lies in her roots. Toni's grandmother, Louis Mary Remington, was born on the Menchin Farm on Waltham Street in Woburn in 1921. Through Toni's exhaustive research, she had discovered much about her Woburn roots:

What I've learned is that Lester Menchin Remington, my grandmother's father, was a Unitarian who married a woman—my great-grandmother Eugenia Louisa Coney—who was Portuguese and a Catholic.

His mother, Fannie Menchin Remington, didn't quite go for that. I know Fannie loved my grandmother, but she would also say very derogatory things about her, because she looked very much like a Portuguese woman. She had dark curly hair and dark eyes, a beautiful child and a beautiful woman.

That beautiful child-woman, who was raised on Waltham Street at the Menchin Farm by Fannie (Menchin) and Charles Remington, married three times, and ended up in Oklahoma City, Oklahoma, where she died in 1982.

On the Remington side of Toni's family is Samuel Kellog Remington, who lived with his wife Ella on 216 Cambridge Street in Woburn and died in 1916. Sam served in the Civil War, where he claimed to have been injured and kept at Libby Prison in New Orleans, Louisiana. Toni, however, turned up some records that contradict that assertion.

He [Sam Remington] spent most of the Civil War in and around New Orleans, LA, where he was injured. After that he was kinda gun shy about going back into combat and got court marshaled for "mutinous conduct" and was imprisoned in Fort Pickens near Barancas, Fla, about the end of 1864. He spent the rest of the Civil War there. About 1865, we find him still awaiting trial. Eventually, they dropped the charges, put him on a ship and sent him back to Boston, because the war had ended.

But Sam's granddaughter, Dorothy Schnelle, comes to his defense. She describes Sam as "very well liked in the neighborhood and kind to the kids. He helped them buy candy, and he used to tell me all kinds of stories." Dorothy lived with Grandpa Sam and wife Ella as a child. In fact, she was there when he died.

As Toni reports:

She said her Grandpa Sam ate lunch and went for a nap. She noticed his glasses had fallen to the floor, and told Grandma Ella. Ella tried to wake him, but told Dorothy that Grandpa Sam would not be waking up anymore. Then she sat quietly in a rocking chair with her Grandma

Ella and spent some time with him after he was gone. Sam was buried in his uniform, and Dorothy said she was so proud she felt her heart would burst.

So it is with those impressive credentials, the power of Toni Lasseter once again compelled the Grave Group to finish what they started back

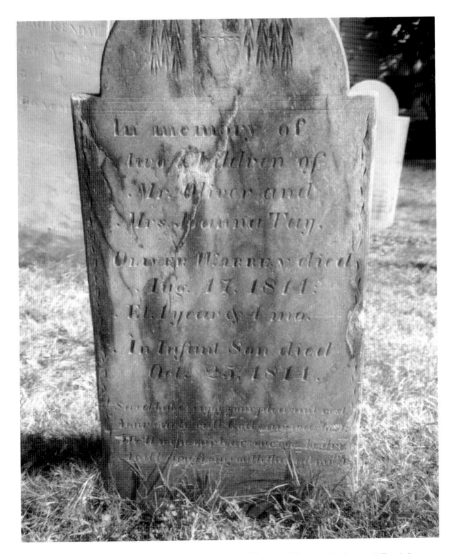

Gravestone of the two infant sons of Oliver and Joanna Tay at the Second Burial Ground, Montvale Avenue, Woburn, Massachusetts. *Courtesy of Gerry Kehoe, Innitou Photo.*

Second Burial Ground gravestone of the children of Dr. Frances and Mrs. Sibil Kittridge, both of whom died in 1808 at eleven and twenty-two months of age. *Courtesy of Gerry Kehoe, Innitou Photo.*

in May 2000. But this time, Toni Lasseter was no longer just a spiritual force on the Internet; she was there in person.

At high noon, the Grave Group partook of a Fitting Feast, made up of foods appropriate for graveyard "al fresco" dining. As the inventory began and each member of the Grave Group fanned out to catalogue a different section of the First Burial Ground, one thing struck them all. When they were done and gathered to compare the lists they had compiled, every member of the Grave Group noted that there were so many children buried there that their ghostly presences could hardly go without special notice.

So it is that the Grave Group would like to dedicate its final day at the Second Burial Ground to the children buried there:

To John Adams, died, April 6, 1832 at age 9 yrs, 3 mos, 2 days; Adrianah Elizabeth Colwell, died April 16, 1832 at age 4 yrs, 9 mos; Sophronia S. Brackett, died May 29, 1832 at age 4 yrs, 3 mos; and her brother John C. Brackett, died May 31, 1832 at age 1 yr, 1 mo; all of whom succumbed to Scarlet Fever in the Spring of 1832.

"Farewell dear babies, 'till the bright morning's rise, Then may we hope to meet thee in the skie." In Memory of two children of Mr. Oliver and Mrs. Joanna Tay; Oliver Warren, died August 17, 1814, Aged 1 year & 4 months. Their infant son died October 25, 1814.

"Sweet babes, enjoy your pleasant rest, Your early call God saw was best; We'll all wipe our tears, our eyes be dry, And learn from you that all must die." Oliver Tay and Joanna Cummings, both of Woburn, were married September 13, 1812. Births of above children not on Woburn Records.

In Memory of two children of Doc't. Francis and Mrs. Sibbil Kittridge; Francis died September 17, 1808, AEt. 11 months & 11 days. Francis D. died September 25, 1814, AEt. 22 months & 28 days.

Children of Dr. Francis Kittridge. The father was admitted member of Woburn First Church, June 1, 1817. The mother was member to same, March 4, 1827. Births of these children not on Woburn Records.

RESTORING BATTLE ROAD'S HUMAN HISTORY

Not too long ago, a visitor from Chicago arrived at our house with a list of historic sites he absolutely had to visit. One was the North Bridge, where the "shot heard 'round the world" was fired on April 19, 1775. And since Minuteman National Historic Park was close by, I volunteered to take him, in spite of the fact that it would be my fourth trip there with out-of-town guests that season.

We found a wonderful park ranger who took our group on a tour of Battle Road Trail, stopping at various points to tell the "human story" of that day in April when so many lives were either lost or changed forever. One tourist was in awe and kept asking the park ranger over and over, "You mean this is the actual road where the Colonial militia pursued the British troops?" And each time the Ranger would assure her it was, and each time she would respond, "Wow!"

At that point, I realized what a treasure that little piece of real estate was and how we locals take it so much for granted. We've built our lives around its history, supplanting historical events with our "human story," and we seem to no longer appreciate its history.

Lexington is not the only community to lay claim to a piece of Battle Road. Woburn has a piece as well, a piece where local "human stories" are embedded in the earth and rocks. One of those "human stories" was told by one of Woburn's West Side residents, who experienced first hand the battle on Lexington Green and lived to tell about it.

On the morning of April 19, 1775, Sylvanus Wood was living at Deacon Kendall's farm at the corner of Cambridge and Locust Streets

Sign marking the beginning of Woburn's Battle Road as it appears today just off
Cambridge Street in Woburn. *Courtesy of the author.*

when he heard the alarm bell. He rose, took up his gun and with Robert
Douglass Sr. and Robert Douglass Jr. hastened along the three miles of
nearby Battle Road that would take him directly to Lexington Green.

The British were still a half-mile from Lexington Green when Wood
arrived, so he joined Captain Parker's men as they lined up to stand firm
against the British. Wood survived the first volley, and then took cover
with the rest. Once the British had moved on to Concord, he returned to
help carry the dead and wounded to the meetinghouse, then proceeded
with the others to Concord.

It was along Battle Road that Wood came across a British soldier
and took him prisoner. That event allowed Wood to claim the honor of
capturing the first British prisoner of the American Revolution. Later, that
title earned him a lifetime pension from the newly formed government of
the United States of America.

Samuel Thompson remembered hearing the alarm between two
o'clock and three o'clock that morning and claims the Woburn
complement started along Battle Road right away, arriving early enough
to fire upon the enemy from Bedford Road in Concord. Although

The retreat from Concord, April 19, 1775.

he described it as a skirmish, three of his company men were killed, including his brother, Daniel Thompson.

Samuel Thompson and his company pursued the British and were close enough behind to shoot at them and see them set fire to houses in Lexington. The company continued onto Concord, then lay in wait for the British to return, pursuing them all the way into Charlestown.

William Tay was with Major Loammi Baldwin and 180 "well-armed townsmen" when they marched along Battle Road from Woburn to Concord. Tay claimed when they reached Lexington Green and saw the carnage that they were "deeply touched," and seeing those bodies "heightened resentment" and spurred the men to pursue the British all the way to Charlestown.

Major Loammi Baldwin was on horseback that day and recorded that he rode along Battle Road ahead of his troops. When he reached Jacob Reed's farm in West Woburn, he heard a "great firing." When he arrived at Lexington, he found eight or ten men lying dead and a number of wounded. Reed's farm was situated in a section of West Woburn known later as Durenville, off Russell Street, about where Stonewall Drive is now and within earshot of Lexington Green.

Indeed, residents of Woburn were surrounded by the sights and sounds of war that day in April, and *The History of Middlesex* records that the "people were stirred by the excitement." Mothers were hard-pressed to comfort their terrified children, and the elderly were reported to feel helpless and full of anxiety. There were also many who experienced grief at the loss of friends and family.

It was not only soldiers who were counted among the dead. Death came as a result of the disease that followed the armies billeted in towns and fields. In fact, the months following that April day brought an epidemic of smallpox that gripped Woburn as the disease spread unchecked. Widow Jane Winn was counted among those who succumbed to smallpox, as well as the child of Benjamin Burnham, Nehemiah Wyman, a nurse and another child, as well as some twenty others who were tended unsuccessfully at Joseph Wyman's house. Records of the day show that during that time, more died of disease than did in battle.

THE BALDWIN–BUNKER HILL CONNECTION

When I first moved to Woburn as a young mother, I felt no particular connection to the city and knew little to nothing about its history. Then one day, as I was pushing a stroller through Woburn Center, I was drawn toward Woburn Common in hopes of learning something about my new home.

As I began to stroll through its memorials and read the signs and plaques posted there, I was surprised and delighted to discover that I'd never really left home. In fact, one plaque proclaimed that Woburn was once part of Charlestown Village, now the Charlestown section of Boston and the neighborhood where I was born and raised.

More recently, I discovered another connection. I learned that the Bunker Hill Monument that loomed over my home along what is now the red line of the Freedom Trail was designed by Woburn's very own Loammi Baldwin II.

My connection to the Bunker Hill Monument is more than geographical; it's emotional as well. As a child, it was the place where I picked dandelions in the spring, rolled down its slopes in summer, collected leaves and acorns in fall and went sledding in winter. The 221-foot summit of that obelisk was also the place my friends and I retreated to on hot summer days, sure to catch a breeze wafting in from the ocean. But most of all, it was the piece of ground where the Revolutionary soldier buried under my bedroom window was mortally wounded.

In researching Baldwin's connection to the Bunker Hill Monument, I also discovered there was some question as to who actually designed

Portrait of Loammi Baldwin II. *Courtesy of Tom Smith.*

the structure. And so did the tenth-grade class at Mount Alvernia High School in Newton, Massachusetts, when they took on an assignment that combined the history and literature of a pre-1800s historic site in Boston. They chose the Bunker Hill Monument, but when trying to determine who created the original design for the monument, they encountered some confusion.

In one instance, the Bunker Hill Monument Association papers mention that Loammi Baldwin of Woburn "decided the 'proportions of the shaft' and created models of the structure in all sizes." Yet another source revealed that it was Horatio Greenough who originated the design, while a third said it was Solomon Willard.

In their final report, after reviewing all the available information, the students of Mount Alvernia High School came to a very fair judgment. They concluded that it was indeed Loammi Baldwin II who designed the Bunker Hill Monument and Solomon Willard who supervised its actual construction. The proof of that can be found in Loammi Baldwin's private letters.

The first mention of the Bunker Hill Monument appears in an April 6, 1825 missive that Baldwin received from the directors of the Bunker Hill Monument Association, informing him he'd been unanimously elected to the association's board, which Baldwin graciously accepted. After several attempts to agree on a meeting date, the very busy Baldwin finally met at Daniel Webster's house to review his "plans and models" for the Bunker Hill Monument.

Finally, on June 7, 1825, the design committee voted on Baldwin's proposed plan. In fact, in his book documenting the contributions of both Loammi Baldwins, Frederick K. Abbott stated that Dr. Joseph Warren, also a member of the planning committee, wrote that the "planning committee stood on the Mill Dam from where Bunker Hill is clearly visible and Baldwin fixed his model to the rails of the dam and stepped back to where the model appeared to be on the hill." Needless to say the committee was impressed.

In his final presentation on July 1, 1825, Baldwin exhibited detailed drawings of his design that showed that the monument would have an "obelisk or pyramid structure" with a square base, 30 feet on each side, narrowing at the top to 15 feet and rising to a height of 220 feet. His drawings also showed that the inside of the obelisk would be hollow, with "circular arches" opening onto a "winding staircase" of 330 steps. Each step would have an eight-inch rise and be one foot deep and two or four

Print of the Bunker Hill Monument, located on Breeds Hill in Charlestown, Massachusetts, shortly after it was dedicated in 1843.

feet in length. And he even provided an estimate of cost (about $100,000), and that figure included "iron lamps, and railings on the staircase." And that pretty much describes the structure that stands there today.

By the time the Bunker Hill Monument was actually under construction in 1842, Loammi Baldwin had passed on and it appears his contributions had been virtually forgotten by the Bunker Hill Monument Association. But Loammi's brother James had not forgotten. As he went through Loammi's papers, he found sufficient evidence that his brother had indeed crafted the original design for the monument, the credit for which was being given to a young college student named Horatio Greenough.

It was then that James set out to see that his brother's unpaid efforts at producing such a magnificent design were correctly attributed to him. He wrote to several of the members of that original planning committee; although some came close to admitting that his brother Loammi did indeed produce the original design for the monument, none would go on record and others skirted the issue completely. By 1852, James allowed the issue to pass, but he and others left behind enough evidence to convince many historians that Loammi Baldwin did indeed design the Bunker Hill Monument.

So it is that the truth has finally been told, and by all present-day accounts, Loammi Baldwin II, the father of American engineering, gets credit for designing the Bunker Hill Monument. But from my perspective, it took a group of high school students to uncover the truth and give credit where credit was due.

(The letters quoted in this chapter are among the collection of Baldwin documents at Harvard University's Baker Library.)

BORN IN THE 1790 HOUSE, 1824–1894

Not too long ago, it was my pleasure to play the role of Eunice Weston Carter Thompson and to act as hostess to the many visitors who stopped by the Eunice Thompson Memorial Library while on the New Bridge Village Tour, sponsored by the Woburn Historical Commission.

What struck me most was the delight and enthusiasm the children took in exploring what some might consider ancient and outdated books, some of which had cobwebs attached to them. But it mattered not. Those children, and everyone else who entered that building, were touched by something that can only be explained as the spirit of love and generosity that Eunice and Jonathan Thompson left behind.

For those of you who were unable to make it that Saturday, let me introduce you to Eunice Thompson and her devoted husband Jonathan, and to the many members of their extended family who have done so much to make Woburn the great city it is today.

I was born Eunice Weston Carter in the 1790 House to Colonel Charles and Eunice Weston Carter of Reading on February 19, 1824, and I was the first child born into the Carter line since 1799. I am descended from Reverend Thomas Carter, who was the first minister of the First Congregational Church in Woburn Center.

My father's family has lived in this part of North Woburn for more than three centuries along the Woburn, Burlington and Wilmington lines. The Carter men provided wood from their woodlots to the Mystic Shipyards and could be seen driving their carts into Charlestown along Main Street at dawn most mornings. In the fall, the Carters brought hops to Charlestown to sell for brewing ale, and also grew and traded this crop so much so that the neighboring towns called this part of Woburn "Hoptown."

I married my childhood sweetheart and dear friend Jonathan Thompson on June 4, 1849. Jonathan and I knew one another quite well. We played in these fields along Elm and Main Streets as children. My mother died when I was fifteen and left behind my sister Lavinia, who was only two years old, and two brothers, whom I raised as my own. Lavinia was my very best friend and remained so right to the end.

Jonathan's father Cyrus lived next door to us at 21 Elm Street most of our married life, and he was a delight. We were fortunate enough to live in Jonathan's grandfather's house (Samuel Thompson), right next door at 31 Elm Street. Samuel kept a diary of his many adventures in the French and Indian and Revolutionary Wars that can be found recorded in *The History of Woburn*, by Samuel Sewell.

Jonathan was descended from one of the original settlers of Woburn, Benjamin Thompson, and we had much in common. Mostly we loved this little village where we spent our lives and felt we wanted to leave something behind to our friends and neighbors that would be lasting.

But Jonathan was adventurous, too. In 1849, he left home and hearth and made his way west to California to take part in the gold rush. He was a genuine Forty-Niner, and although some thought it strange that he left his wife behind to go on such a venture, I supported him wholeheartedly.

I passed on May 5, 1894, at age seventy. I understand friends and family were gracious enough to remember me as a kind, gentle, cheerful and even-tempered woman and that Jonathan found me to be a devoted wife. But that last year before I passed, I suffered greatly. I was comforted by so many friends and family who stopped by each day to keep my spirits high. It was a delight to see them, and they made me smile.

There was much weeping at my funeral, and many tears were shed for the passing of a "dear wife, sister and friend." Many could not believe one so good could be gone from this earth. I am humbled by their kind words.

In 1899, Jonathan's old Forty-Niner friends came and all celebrated their fiftieth reunion together and talked endlessly of their adventures. Jonathan came to join me a year later on August 27, 1900, and his funeral was held in our home. He was carried to Woodbrook Cemetery, where he was laid to rest. Before Jonathan died, he instructed the executers of his will to use this piece of land where we used to play as children and that the family had earlier leased to the city for a one-room schoolhouse and for the building of a library.

The Eunice Memorial Library on Elm Street in what was known as the New Bridge Village section of Woburn. *Courtesy of the author.*

Finally, Jonathan's will was settled and the amount of $17,000 was set aside to build this wonderful library and make it available to everyone in New Bridge Village, especially to the children, as they had difficulty making their way into Woburn Center to visit the library there. The library was officially opened in 1906, and I'm honored to have it dedicated in my name—the Eunice Thompson Memorial Library.

Much to my delight, a cousin of mine, Frances Parkinson Wheeler, went on to become the famous author, Frances Parkinson Keyes. But she was only nine years old the last time I saw her at one of our family gatherings at the 1790 House. I knew her when she was just a small girl with a great sense of adventure. She would come to Woburn to visit her grandmother for whom she was named at the 1790 House. She loved exploring that old house and once in awhile she would come visit me. It gives me such pleasure that she may have come to visit this library and now I understand we have all her books housed here.

Young Frances was my cousin through my Carter relatives. Her father was raised in the 1790 House when his father, Reverend Melancthon Wheeler,

Sign marking the Eunice Thompson Memorial Library when it was dedicated in 1906.

came to be the pastor of the North Congregational Church in 1865. At that time, the parsonage was at the 1790 House. Another reason for his being in Woburn was that his son John, who was young Frances's father, was a brilliant student and had won a scholarship to attend the prestigious Warren Academy on Warren Avenue, now the site of New Horizons.

Poor little Frances never knew what a wonderful man her father was—her time with him was brief. He died suddenly at the age of thirty-six, shortly after young Frances was born. His heart just gave out and many said it was because he was always studying and never took part in any exercise that would have made his heart stronger.

On the day little Frances was born, her grandmother was so delighted to have a healthy grandchild that she sat down and wrote Frances the most wonderful letter welcoming her into the world. Frances was so taken by that letter it became her dearest possession. The letter was addressed to her from the 1790 House in "N. Woburn, Mass., July 29, 1885," and can be read in its entirety in young Frances's autobiography, *Roses in December.*

I remember watching from my window here at 31 Elm Street as Frances would run with abandon through the fields with her three male Carter cousins. It was such a pleasure to see her enjoying this open piece of land. And now, to have her come visit as one of the world's most famous authors is something I could never have dreamed. Her most famous book is *Dinner at Antoine's,* but that came only a close second to her 1950 bestseller, *Joy Street*. Some of her other works are *Came a Cavalier*, *The Chess Player* and *Old Gray Homestead*.

The last time Frances was at the 1790 House was when she was about eleven years old. She and another cousin of mine, Ruel Carter, had an adventure there that Frances wrote about in her autobiography. She and Ruel were on a hunt to find a fireplace hidden way up in the attic. It was a place where runaway slaves were hidden to keep them from being returned to their slave owners. Frances and Ruel, who were only a year apart in age, risked life and limb to climb up onto the rafters and across the ceiling to find it. They were so excited by their discovery they could talk of nothing else. That summer at the 1790 House was so memorable to young Frances; she used it as the setting for one of her novels, entitled *A Rebel Captain's Sweetheart*.

Frances married Wilder Keyes in 1903 when she was only eighteen and moved to New Hampshire. She was fifteen when my darling husband Jonathan died, and she came to join us in 1970 at the age of eighty-five. Now Jonathan and I are surrounded by so many of our family and friends that we are eternally happy, and we look down with pride at the gift we were able to bestow on our wonderful city of Woburn and hope future generations will forever cherish the Eunice Thompson Memorial Library, as well as the homes of our ancestors on Elm Street.

CHRISTMAS BURGLARIES, CIRCA 1859

It was two nights before Christmas and all through the neighboring towns, creatures were stirring. But a lengthy newspaper report in the *Woburn Weekly Budget* of December 23, 1859, described that stirring as anything but an early visit from Santa. In fact, they headlined their story: "Systematic Roguery."

It seems a "band of desperate thieves" had been burglarizing homes and businesses in Woburn, Winchester and West Cambridge all through the holiday season. So much so that the editor of the *Budget* advised everyone to arm themselves at all times. Unfortunately, the hired man that worked for Stephen Swan in West Cambridge, right on the Winchester line, didn't get the message in time.

Swan's handyman had been tasked with guarding over his home while the family was visiting relatives for the holidays when there arose a clatter in the barn. He "sprang from his bed to see what was the matter" and bumped into two men turning the cattle out into the cold December night. But just in the nick of time, he managed to chase the rogues off.

In the process, he noticed they had saddled up one of Swan's horses with the intention of herding the cattle off into the night. He added that, unlike Santa's reindeer, the fact that one of Swan's bovines had a shiny nose didn't mean that any of them could fly.

If that incident were not enough to scare off Santa's reindeer, a hired man on duty at another home in Winchester bumped into some Grinches that were about to heat up the holidays. He was just about to make his appointed rounds when he was viciously clubbed over the head and set upon by ruffians. This time, the owners were nearby and when they heard the commotion, they set out to investigate. That's when they found the poor man down and out for the count.

While the women of the house tended to his wounds, the men headed for the barn to check on the reindeer—I mean, livestock. When they reached the barn, they found that the burglars had added a bit of Christmas cheer to the season by setting it on fire. Seems the ruffians had flown out of sight before anyone could catch a glimpse of them, but this time the homeowners were determined to get proof. And instead of leaving out cookies in hopes that the evil elves might leave behind some DNA, they offered a $500 reward for the "conviction of the rogues."

It wasn't long before those very rogues made their way to Woburn and targeted the estate of Jacob Pierce on Cambridge Road, just about where Horn Pond Plaza is now. But the boldness of this particular robbery caused everyone to think that maybe there was someone besides Santa that knew their way around the family home. This time it appeared that

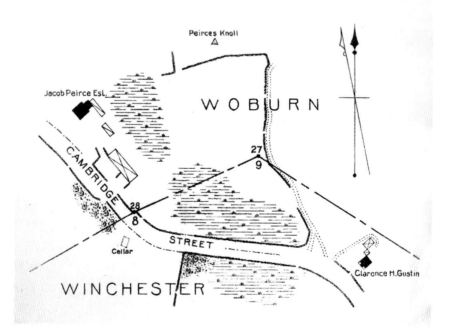

Map of the Jacob Pierce Estate off Cambridge Street in Woburn near the Winchester line. *Boundary Lines of Woburn, 1899.*

not only did the robbers know the floor plan, they also chose the exact day that Pierce had collected on several debts and his wallet was full of Christmas cheer. In fact, it had several hundred dollars worth of gold coins in it, as well as a note for $1,000.

As reported in the newspaper both the coins and the note were taken from his pants pocket in the middle of the night. Well actually the entire pocket was stolen. All of which made the police suspicious that the thieves had more than a familiarity with Mr. Pierce because they snuck into his bedroom in the middle of the night and cut the pocket out of his pants while he was sleeping nearby. They even returned a short time later to steal his watch and some silver from the dining room—all of which pointed to an inside job.

Having these robberies occur so close to Christmas made for anything but a festive holiday season. The first burglary was just coming to light when the Haywood family of Winchester returned home from gobbling Thanksgiving turkey at their relatives' house and found their home had been ransacked. This led the police to believe that, unlike the Pierce robberies, these rogues were unfamiliar with the Heywood's floor plan.

The rash of burglaries spread to local businesses when it was discovered that Woburn's Lyceum Hall had been broken into, as well as a store belonging to a Mr. J. Hovey in Winchester. But police were beginning to connect the dots when A.A. Parsons, an express man living on Bow Street in Woburn, had his house broken into. This time the thieves not only took Parson's wallet, they relieved him of his express book, which led police to believe the burglars were probably trying to figure out Santa's route ahead of time so they could meet up with him in person and relieve him of all those heavy packages.

Things seemed to be spiraling out of control when police received a report from someone who had overheard a conversation on Woburn Common that led them to believe that the rogues were expanding their operation. The gist of the conversation was that there had been a pickpocket working the crowd that had gathered to hear a "pill doctor" make his pitch about his miracle cure (for just about everything but robbery). But what stunned everyone was that even the pill doctor had his pocket picked and was now missing his silver watch and chain.

It wasn't long before Woburn, Winchester and Boston police caught up with that gang of thieves and found that it was made up of four local men, two of whom were found with the goods still on them. When confronted with the evidence, they had no choice but to confess to the

Woburn Common at the unveiling of the Soldiers Monument, circa 1865. *Courtesy of John McElhiney.*

robberies; it was also of no surprise to anyone that two of them were named Pierce—John and Franklin.

The other two, George Tisdale and William Hutchinson, were able to come up with the $4,000 bail and were released until trial. But no one came forward to rescue the Pierces from the jaws of justice and they were held in prison until such time as they could be held accountable by a jury.

That occurred just in time for Christmas, when a grand jury proceeding brought together several witnesses to testify against the defendants on the day before Christmas. When the final verdict was rendered, Santa came through for William Hutchinson and John Pierce and their cases were dismissed on a technicality. But Frank Pierce and George Tisdale woke up to a stocking full of coal when it was determined that there was enough evidence against them to be held over for trial.

In any case, most left the courthouse just in time to enjoy hanging up their stockings with care. Unfortunately, there was no follow-up news story to tell who got coal and who didn't, but if I come across one, I'll certainly share it with you.

HORN POND, DEADLY POND

The twentieth century heralded the birth of quantum physics and the automobile, yet many people held fast to myths and superstitions. One of the superstitions of that time was attached to the swirling, dark waters of Horn Pond. Many Woburnites at the turn of the century were convinced that demons in the depths of Horn Pond somehow exacted tribute from its residents. They believed that the pond took a life each year, and if it skipped a year, it took two the next. And who could blame them. Between 1870 and 1890, Horn Pond had swallowed the life force of twenty-three victims.

Although records of drownings in Horn Pond prior to 1870 are sparse, there were nine documented. The first was that of Mrs. James Converse in 1803, yet little is noted other than the date and cause of death.

In August of 1861, Timothy Holland, who was in the employ of Pierce & Hall ice dealers, also found the waters of Horn Pond waiting greedily for him when he stood up in his boat, fell in and was immediately sucked to the bottom. What makes his accident stand out among others was that it claimed the life of Mrs. Ellen Mosher also, in spite of the fact she was safely on shore. It seems Mrs. Mosher, recently emigrated from Ireland, was so overcome by the tragedy that she "was thrown into convulsive fits which resulted in her death a few hours later."

Young William Menard is also one of Horn Pond's victims. Menard was just a lad of fourteen when he decided to take two of his Lexington Street neighbors fishing on a stiflingly hot day in July 1869. Since his friends were much younger than he, he probably promised their mothers to keep a good eye on them. That is most likely why, when one of his charges lost the float off his line, William volunteered to wade in to get it. Unfortunately, he was surprised by the sudden drop off into sixteen feet of deep water and sank below the surface, leaving his younger charges on shore yelling for help. But help arrived too late, and days later William's classmates filed into church benches in an orderly fashion for his funeral, led by their teacher, Mr. Perkins.

Like many of the pond's victims, Louis Bournique and Michael McNamara were doing nothing more harmful than seeking relief on a sultry August day, Louis in 1864 and Michael in 1869. Although five years separated their drownings, each had a similar experience. Bournique and McNamara merely waded in to cool off and found themselves in very deep water. It seems the shoreline had been prepared by the ice companies for the landing of ice in winter. To accomplish this, they dredged the bottom of the pond a few feet from shore, causing a sudden drop off and putting bathers at risk. Bournique and McNamara slipped into one of these deep holes and breathed no more.

As tragic as the fourteen reported deaths that occurred in the years preceding 1877 were, none stands out as horrendously as the event that occurred on July 4, 1877, in sight of hundreds of picnickers, boaters and bathers celebrating the Fourth of July at Horn Pond. It was on that occasion that five people, including a six-year-old boy, drowned in full view of helpless onlookers. Even more tragic was the fact that four of the victims belonged to the same family.

Dennis O'Leary had arrived at the pond to celebrate the Fourth with eight members of his family. He and a friend, Thomas Kenney, decided to rent a boat at Cormack's boathouse in Town Cove. After securing the boat, he and Kenney went to pick up the remaining family members, piling nine more people into the sixteen-foot rowboat. Among them were his wife, Anna Rossiter O'Leary, their two small children, his brother-in-law Lawrence Rossiter, Lawrence's wife Bridget, their three youngsters and a young female friend, Anne Curran, thus overloading the boat with eleven people.

Eyewitnesses described seeing one of the men stand as if to switch places to take his turn at rowing. Just then, he tripped and fell, tipping the boat completely over and dumping all eleven occupants into twenty feet of water. Alexander Cormack, Fred Bryant and Daniel Barnum went immediately to the rescue and pulled Lawrence Rossiter and two of his children to safety along with Anne Curran and the two O'Leary children.

Dennis (b. 1852) and Ann Rossiter O'Leary (b. 1850) drowned in Horn Pond, July 4, 1877, leaving behind two orphaned sons. *Courtesy of the Nisco Family Collection.*

Norma Nisco and sons Michael and Philip, great-great-grandsons of Dennis and Ann O'Leary. *Courtesy of the Nisco Family Collection.*

But the deaths of Dennis and Anna O'Leary and Bridget Rossiter left two children motherless and two others orphaned.

What is most remarkable about this story is that it continues today. Recently, Norma Nisco of Fountain Valley, California, contacted the Woburn Public Library, seeking documentation of a story told by her grandfather of that Fourth of July family tragedy. It turns out her grandfather, Michael Joseph O'Leary, was one of the surviving O'Leary children who had been plucked from the grip of Horn Pond that day. In the flurry of mail, both electronic and snail, more details from family members put a human face on an event that occurred over 120 years ago.

According to Norma Nisco, the only reason her grandfather and his older brother survived was because they were wearing dresses, as was the custom for very young children of the day. These dresses filled with air and held the two young boys, ages one and three, aloft, keeping them bobbing like little corks until rescuers could get to them.

Left an orphan, Michael Joseph O'Leary was taken in by James and Elizabeth Canniff of Winchester, a couple in their fifties with six children of their own. By 1880, the Canniffs had adopted Michael. It is believed the other O'Leary son went to live with the Rossiters in Milford, New Hampshire.

Michael O'Leary Canniff went on to marry Sarah Hickey of Woburn. It is believed there was a special bond between Sarah and Michael right from the beginning as Sarah had lost her brother, Thomas Hickey, to the depths of the pond on July 4, 1878, exactly one year after Horn Pond had made Michael an orphan.

Thomas Hickey was drowned at age eleven, attempting to save his little friend, Patrick Murphy, age eight. The medical examiner carried Hickey's limp, lifeless body to his Fowle Street home, etching a lasting image on the then four-year-old Sarah's memory. Patrick Murphy survived.

Lawrence Rossiter, who lost his wife and one of his three children in that July Fourth tragedy, married Anne Curran, the young woman who had been plucked from the jaws of death with him, in August of 1877.

Michael and Mary Hickey, parents of Thomas Hickey, who drowned in Horn Pond July 4, 1878, and Sarah Hickey, who married Michael O'Leary Canniff. *Courtesy of the Nisco Family Collection.*

Rossiter family with Dennis O'Leary Canniff, his wife Sara (Hickey) and their daughter Annette on Rossiter Farm in Milford, New Hampshire, circa 1920. *Courtesy of the Nisco Family Collection.*

Norma Nisco made sure to offer her thanks to the ancestors of Alexander Cormack, Fred Bryant and Daniel Barnum, the men who rescued her grandfather. By all accounts, Michael Joseph O'Leary Canniff was a wonderful, loving, caring man who took in many family members when in need, returning the favor done him by the Canniffs many times over.

Drowning at Horn Pond was not always accidental. Many desperate souls chose the murky depths of the pond as their last resting place. One family living on Buck Street in the 1880s suffered more than any from the melancholy depression that sent so many to seek permanent relief in the pond's cooling waters.

On August 2, 1882, Bartholomew Lombard's brother Patrick reported him missing. Lombard and his wife Catherine shared their home with Bartholomew and became concerned when he failed to come home the previous evening. But it was five whole days before Wade, engineer for the Woburn Water Works, spotted a body one hundred yards from the shore of the pumping station.

When the body was retrieved, it was identified as Bartholomew Lombard. The body had some some minor scratches and bruises on it, but the medical examiner deemed his death a suicide, and the family didn't object.

Some two years later, on August 14, 1884, Catherine Lombard left home at 5:00 a.m. and two hours later was found drowned at the foot of Richardson Street. Her death was also judged a suicide and attributed to her poor health of recent years.

As if this were not enough tragedy for the Lombard family to absorb, on July 22, 1886, Patrick Lombard decided to end his life in the same way. But as fate would have it, Mr. W.J. Nelson of Winchester just happened by in time to save him. Lombard must have been terribly distraught as he was immediately taken into protective custody by the police.

No sooner was Patrick released from custody than he once again threw himself into the pond and once again was saved, but Patrick was determined and decided to take a different course of action. On May 19, 1887, he climbed to the top of Mount Misery and slashed his throat, hoping at last for some release from his private torment, but once again he was discovered and saved. He was taken to the almshouse on top of Rag Rock, where his wounds were dressed, and he was released.

No record of Patrick's final demise is recorded in obituary accounts, so it is not known if he finally succeeded in escaping his tormented life by his own hand.

Between 1890 and 1945, eighteen more citizens were claimed by the pond. From fourteen-year-old Patrick Ryan, who came to celebrate the Fourth of July in 1906 and disappeared in the old "swimmin' hole," to twenty-year-old Arthur Gage, honor student and Class Prophet (class of 1906), who along with friends dove off their boat to swim to Horn Pond Island and immediately sank out of sight, to the unidentified man whose body was found in September of 1942, floating twenty feet from the pumping station, the pond continued to claim victims and, to some minds, sacrifices.

One particularly tragic drowning occurred on July 26, 1943, when three young girls disappeared "without utterance or outcry" into the deep water fifty yards from Horn Pond brook bridge. Only one girl in a group of four was saved by the valiant efforts of lifeguard Joseph Giffune when he pulled thirteen-year-old Lillian Zercon to safety.

Giffune had arrived on duty a little earlier than usual and was getting the boat from the pumping station to patrol the pond. He heard shouts from shore and saw struggling in the water a short distance away. He went in the water, clothes and all, and pulled Zercon to safety. He and lifeguard Alvin Breyton continued their rescue attempt but were only able to recover the lifeless body of thirteen-year-old Evelyn Hooper from the determined waters of the pond. Later in the day, the bodies of Loretta Zebrauski (age ten) and Mildred Cooper (age eleven) were retrieved.

Distraught parents and family members clung to each other in their sorrow at joint funeral services at the Methodist church in Woburn, where Mildred Ruth Cooper and Evelyn Jean Hooper were wished a fond farewell. Loretta Zebrauski, who had come to visit with her cousin, Lillian Zercon, was buried in her hometown of Lawrence.

In 1964, Foley Beach was moved to the parkway side of the pond and continued to offer residents a safe swimming environment with lifeguards on duty. But when a survey was done in 1984, it was discovered that only 18 percent of the bathers were Woburn residents. Due to those findings and budget cuts, it was decided the beach would be closed and no swimming would be allowed at the pond.

We can never be sure if our turn-of-the-century ancestors were right in concluding that demons in the depths of Horn Pond demanded human sacrifices, or whether we just got a lot smarter about water safety. But it is certain that, in modern times, the pond has claimed fewer and fewer victims each succeeding year. That could also be because each year fewer and fewer are foolish enough tempt the spirit of Horn Pond.

Victims of Horn Pond Drownings

1803: Mrs. James Converse
1846: Martha Hood
1859: Catherine Ryan
1860: Thomas Cutler
1861: Nancy Edgerly and Timothy Holland
1864: Louis Bournique
1867: Michael McNamara
1869: William Menard
1870: Charles Luke Riley and George Doherty
1871: Maggie McIntire
1876: Redmond Owens and Frank Maxwell

1877: Dennis O'Leary, Anna Rossiter O'Leary, Thomas Kenney, Robert Rossiter, Bridget Rossiter and James Daley
1878: Thomas Hickey
1881: Thomas Kelley
1882: Bartholomew Lombard
1884: Catherine Lombard and Abbie Davis Fay
1885: Michael McDermot Jr.
1886: Joseph McDermott
1889: Webster Potter
1890: Jessie Croucher, Etta Parr, Edward O'Rourke and Mary Darmody
1905: Michael Ryan
1906: Arthur Gage
1909: Dr. Wilford D. McDonald
1914: Joseph McGarrity
1916: Jeremiah Shea
1919: George McNeil Jr.
1924: Jeremiah Shea
1932: Francis J. McMurray, Patrick O'Donnell and Frank McKinnon
1938: Coleman Connolly
1940: Henry McDonald
1942: unidentified man
1943: Loretta Zebrauski
1943: Mildred R. Cooper
1943: Evelyn Hooper
1945: Maxine Catania

This list was compiled from *Woburn Deaths 1642–1900* and newspaper accounts.

Harvesting Ice on Horn Pond was "Warm Work"

Winter's mild temperatures in recent years make it difficult to envision the ice harvesting that took place on Horn Pond for more than a century. In fact, these last few winters would most definitely have put the ice companies that hugged the shores of Horn Pond out of business in a hurry. But between 1820 and 1920, the ice business on Horn Pond boomed.

Not all of Woburn's early immigrants worked in the tanneries. Many sought employment in the equally thriving ice industry. In fact, Woburn's Horn Pond, along with Lake Quannapowitt in Wakefield and Suntang Lake in Lynnfield, was among the major ice suppliers in Massachusetts that delivered their cargo to Boston to be packed in cargo ships and exported to ports all along the Atlantic coast, as well as to exotic ports all over the world.

History records that it was William Fletcher, born in 1770, who was the first person to deliver a cartload of "ice into Boston for merchandise." But the idea of creating an industry from the production and sale of ice seemed as bizarre an idea back in the early 1800 as the production and sale of the air we breathe would be today.

In fact, when a brash Massachusetts entrepreneur, Frederick Tudor, set out to make his fortune in the ice trade in 1806, a Boston newspaper scoffed at the idea and joked that it was a "slippery speculation." Tudor's plan to become the "Ice King" became the butt of many a joke in business circles, but his eventual success prompted many other entrepreneurs to turn local lakes and ponds into ice-producing cash cows.

Ice cutting on Horn Pond, 1896. *Courtesy of John McElhiney.*

Firsthand accounts of ice harvesting, as it was done for more than a century before its mechanization in the 1930s and 1940s, are few and far between. Only a few imperfect accounts of those early methods were handed down. The icemen who worked in bitterly cold temperatures scraping, planing, marking ice for plowing, sawing (or "baring off") the floats and poling those five-ton blocks toward the icehouse elevator for storage weren't ones who wrote books or kept diaries. The life of an iceman was a hard one. It was not a form of employment many revered enough to record, although there are a few authentic sources that help the reader experience what ice harvesting was really like between 1800 and 1920.

According to Parker Converse, in his book *Legends of Woburn*, it was Jonathan Gillis who was the first to harvest and commercially sell ice cut from Horn Pond in 1825. But local farmers had been coming regularly to the pond for supplies of ice to preserve fruit and vegetables through the summer months.

In fact, an article appearing in the Essex Institute Historical Collections in 1961, entitled "Crystal Blocks of Yankee Coldness," mentions a "curious sideline of the ice-trade." It seems New England Baldwin apples, first grown in Woburn, were "shipped in barrels among blocks of ice" all the way to India. It seems the English became so hooked on them they were willing to pay as much as seventy-five cents for one apple, which made the export of Baldwin apples a very profitable trade.

Even before Jonathan Gillis cut his first piece of ice to sell, the Horn Pond House on Arlington Road, then Canal Street, harvested ice every winter beginning in 1820. It stored it away for the use of their guests throughout the busy summer months. But it wasn't until 1853 that Daniel Draper and Sons built ten icehouses on the southern end of Horn Pond that the ice-cutting business was taken up in earnest. That year Draper and Sons harvested fifty thousand tons of ice.

The next year, 1854, when the railroad along the old Middlesex Canal route was completed, the ice business boomed and other ice companies saw the wisdom of setting up businesses along Horn Pond's shores. With companies like the Boston Ice Company and Hall & Pierce, who had unlimited funds to invest in the business, the ice business became one of Woburn's major employers.

Men looking for work would line up every morning at dawn to be picked for a crew that would work from dawn until dusk, seven days a week, during harvesting season. At the end of each day, they were paid the princely sum of one dollar. Hall & Pierce alone employed more than one hundred men to harvest the ice, over and above the usual crew that maintained the icehouses during the remainder of the year.

Major Thomas Pierce, whose home is still standing at the corner of Lake Avenue and Main Street, was an expert in the ice business following

Boston & Lowell locomotive (1883) similar to the one that traveled the spur along the old Middlesex Canal and moved ice to Boston. *Courtesy of the Woburn Historical Commission.*

in the footsteps of relative Elmore Pierce, who had been a local ice cutter supplying Woburn with ice every summer for many years.

One summer in August of 1861, one of Hall & Pierce's employees met an untimely end when he drowned in Horn Pond. It seems Timothy Holland and Michael Reagan borrowed one of Hall & Pierce's boats to row across the pond to meet friends at Thompson Village. About 5:00 p.m., while on their way back, Holland stood up in the boat, lost his balance and fell over the side. Reagan went back for him, but when Holland popped back up he was unsuccessful in grabbing onto him.

Reagan rowed furiously to the supply shed at the icehouse, grabbed some poles and hooks and went back to look for Holland. But it was too late. All he could retrieve from the black water was the lifeless body of his friend Timothy Holland. Since Holland lived near the icehouses, word spread quickly and a crowd gathered. One neighbor, Mrs. Mosher, whose husband James worked with Holland at Hall & Pierce, became so distraught that she suffered a stroke and died a few hours later.

During the 1913 ice-harvesting season, another tragedy struck, but this time it was of the animal variety. According to the *Woburn Journal*, a thirteen-hundred-pound horse belonging to the Horn Pond Ice Company was being worked by a crew at 3:30 a.m., scraping the snow off the ice to prepare it for cutting, when the poor beast plummeted through the ice and drowned—in spite of the rope workers had secured around its neck in case of such an event. But at thirteen hundred pounds, the massive equine sank like a rock in forty feet of water, proving too heavy for the crew to rescue.

The activity at Horn Pond during ice-harvesting time drew crowds of onlookers from all over who came to watch the unique scene. The sight of men floating cakes of ice three feet square through open channels of water toward the icehouses, where they were lifted onto ramps that carried them to the top of a tower, made for a colorful pageant. But it's hard to believe the icemen of long ago would describe their work as colorful. As one worker reported facetiously, "It was warm work."

Unmasking the "Yeggmen"

During one of the many conversations with my friend Ruth Boyden, who passed away in 2004 only a few months before her 105th birthday, she used a term that intrigued me. She referred to "yeggmen" as having committed terrible crimes in Woburn when she was a child. But when I pressed her further, she had little to add. After all, she was only nine years old in 1908 when the "yeggmen" made their appearance in the area.

I made a note of the term and promised myself that someday I would find out what it meant, or if there really were "yeggmen," or if it was merely the overworked imagination of a nine-year-old girl. After all, the term came close to bogeymen, so I wasn't quite sure yeggmen existed at all. But recently I've uncovered some proof that yeggmen did indeed exist, and that they were every bit as scary as bogeymen.

First of all, you need to understand the meaning and origin of the word "yeggmen," and who better to explain that than Allan Pinkerton, the first real-life private eye in America. Pinkerton founded the Pinkerton Detective Agency shortly after the Civil War and his sons continued the enterprise, building it into the largest detective agency in the world.

According to a speech given by Allan Pinkerton's son William in 1900, the Pinkerton Detective Agency was well aware of "yeggmen," a term it seems that originated from the gypsy culture and was used to designate the cleverest thief in the gypsy tribe. The term "yegg" meant "chief thief" and yeggmen were in evidence wherever gypsies set up camp.

But around the turn of the twentieth century, a new dimension was added when a more sophisticated thief took on the term and gave it new meaning. This new breed of yeggmen was very organized. Their method of operation was to send out someone they termed a "gay cat" to case small towns. The gay cat would pose as a beggar, and in order to elicit sympathy from the unsuspecting locals he would pour creosote on his arm between his elbow and his wrist to produce what looked like a freshly inflicted wound. They called this tactic "jigging."

Some of the things the gay cat looked for were whether the town had electricity, a police force on duty all night or a night watchman at the bank, as well as who carried large sums of money after dark. Then the gay cat would report back to the other yeggmen, and they would plan their operation accordingly.

Most of their nefarious activities were conducted after dark, when they would come into small towns in groups to execute their plan to rob a bank or attack unsuspecting businesspeople along the highway whom they believed were carrying large sums of money. But on February 6, 1908, something went very wrong with the yeggmen's plan and what ensued was a vast manhunt that included most area police forces and the men of Company G, the area's army unit stationed at the Woburn Armory.

It all began when Officers Walsh and O'Neil observed three suspicious-looking men crossing onto the Woburn Common from the Unitarian Church on the corner of Winn Street. When the officers shouted for the men to stop, they began to run and the officers took off after them. With the officers close in on their heels, the fugitives turned

Officers Timothy Walsh and Edward O'Neil (sixth, seventh from left), who were shot by "yeggmen," and Officer Bernard Murphy (eleventh from left), who pursued them, 1912. *Courtesy of John McElhiney.*

onto Church Avenue, and at that point the group of yeggmen turned as one and fired a volley of shots, felling both Walsh and O'Neil, something yeggmen referred to as "jimmying a bull," or shooting an officer.

What the officers didn't know was that the yeggmen had just waylaid two businessmen in Billerica near Pinehurst Park and were now making their way back to escape on the train to Boston. When they got near the B&M tracks, they encountered outraged citizen Bert Donahue, who grabbed one of them by the coat; a yeggman fired five shots and Donahue sank injured to the ground.

By then Officer Murphy had joined the chase and reached the spot where Donahue was downed. It was at that point that the yeggmen split up, one heading toward Warren Avenue and Sturgis Street while the other two took off up Lexington Street toward the West Side.

Officer Murphy chose to continue his pursuit of the yeggman who had shot at Donahue and who had already reached the summit of Academy Hill on Warren Avenue. But before Murphy could get close enough to grab him, the desperate yeggman encountered Sherwood Van Tassel, a young boy of twelve out on an errand for his mother. It's not known if the boy just took him by surprise or if he tried to impede him in anyway, but what is known is that the fugitive pulled out his automatic weapon and let off a fusillade of shots, sending the boy reeling with a bullet to his leg.

At the same time, Officer Keating, having information that the other two yeggmen had been seen on Lexington Street, commandeered a cart driven by Edward Holland and ordered Holland to take off after them. When Officer Keating spotted the two men along the road in front of the Dobbins and Shannon farm, he ordered them to stop. Instead they turned and fired a volley of shots, hitting the innocent Holland in the back and seriously injuring him.

Back in Woburn Center, crowds gathered in front of the police station, where Mayor Blodgett announced he had called on Company G for volunteers to assist the police in their manhunt. It was now 3:30 a.m. when the men of Company G headed toward Winning Farm, where the suspects were last seen. They spread out and combed the area all the way to Arlington Heights and Lexington Center, where they were joined in the hunt by Lexington and Arlington police.

At dawn that morning, it was announced that two of the yeggmen had been captured in Arlington, and another, not directly involved in the Woburn incident, had been taken prisoner in Chelsea. But the fugitive

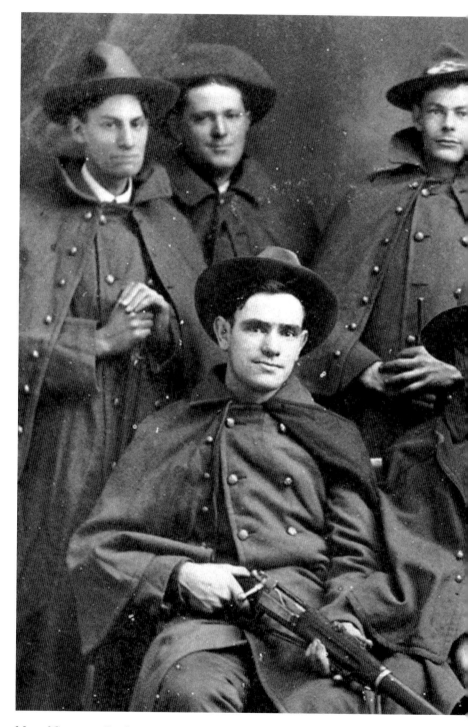

Men of Company G, who answered the call in the pursuit of the "yeggmen," circa 1910. *Courtesy of John McElhiney.*

most wanted by police, the one who had shot twelve-year-old Sherwood Van Tassel, had escaped.

The good news was that all of the victims who were shot so callously by the yeggmen survived, and the three yeggmen who were captured were found guilty and sent to state prison for twenty-five years. Beyond that success, the case remained unsolved.

But in 1911, when Boston police extradited three fugitives—one from Russia and two others from Austria—who had been charged with robbing a jewelry store in Boston, area police began to have hope of closing the case out completely. What gave them hope was that one of the suspects was believed to be a relative of the yeggman who had escaped after shooting young Sherwood Van Tassel, and police hoped they could convince him to reveal where he was hiding.

By this time, police had identified the shooter as Chris Zeltin and issued a $500 reward for his capture that was still in effect. Now area police held out some hope of actually capturing and prosecuting the yeggman who had escaped their grasp in 1908. But so far, I've found no further information that would lead me to believe that they were able to bring Chris Zeltin to justice. I am thus left to believe that he remained at large either in the United States or in Russia, and that his attack on an unsuspecting young boy of twelve went unpunished.

WOBURN ROOMING HOUSE MURDERS

Murder and mayhem was rampant in Woburn from the late 1800s through the turn of the century. Woburn's boom times brought hordes of people to live in close quarters and get on each other's nerves, like Joseph Hurst and Dennis Meagher.

Dennis Meagher was described in news reports as a gas fitter and a well-developed twenty-three-year-old about five feet ten inches tall. Although his friend and constant companion, John Chambers, shared the same age and occupation, he was of a more imposing stature, at six feet three inches tall. Chambers and Meagher were plumbers who came from Boston to Woburn to work at Messrs. Buel & Flint in the fall of 1873. They took up residence in a boardinghouse on Mann Street owned and operated by Mr. and Mrs. Joseph Hurst, described as English and therefore of "quiet and well behaved character."

On the other hand, Chambers and Meagher were anything but "quiet and well behaved." It seems they made no end of a nuisance of themselves, insulting anyone who crossed their paths and claiming that they would "clean out the insignificant town of Woburn."

In the process of fulfilling their threat, they pushed Mr. Hurst too far when they insulted Mrs. Hurst, using vulgar and profane language and refusing to leave the boardinghouse when ordered out. This prompted Mr. Hurst to whistle for the police, forcing the altercation out the front door, where Mr. Hurst declared he would protect home and hearth and produced a pistol to put some bite in his bark.

That didn't deter Dennis Meagher. He pretended to put his hand in his pocket and instead drew back and punched Hurst in the face. Hurst fired his revolver, supposedly in the air, but claims that his hand was deflected by Meagher's blow, and the shot hit Meagher in the abdomen. Meagher didn't immediately appear wounded, as he ran about one hundred yards before he fell. He later succumbed to his injuries at 2:00 p.m. on October 7, 1873.

What followed was a coroner's inquest where all the principles made statements, and the jury decided that Hurst had not intentionally shot Meagher and discharged him from custody. This didn't sit well with Meagher's sister, who arrived from Boston full of fire and brimstone demanding a grand jury be convened to look into her brother's untimely death. When that jury failed to see justice done as she demanded, she brought a civil suit against the Hursts to recover damages for causing the loss of her brother. It wasn't long before that civil suit was also dismissed for lack of merit and Ms. Meagher walked away with nothing to show for her effort.

The very next year, in July of 1874, another boardinghouse fatality occurred over on the westerly side of Rag Rock off Bedford Street in the section of Woburn known then as Cummingsville. But this fatality hardly lived up to the sensational headline given it by the *Woburn Advertiser*.

"HOMICIDE, ARSON, AND BURGLARY" the paper's headline shouted, under an even larger headline that read: "THE WORKS OF RUM." Although rum did play a part in the death of John McCourd, it was more of a tragedy than a cold-blooded murder.

McCourd was a quiet man of thirty-seven years old who had lost his wife three weeks before and was struggling to earn money to raise a young child. He was employed as a "beamster" at the Cummings tannery and just happened to be in the wrong place at the wrong time.

That place was the Bouviard boardinghouse where, on the night of July 25, 1874, a melee ensued when a group of rowdies came to the house demanding beer. Bouviard sold them each a glass for five cents. When they got too rowdy, he asked them to leave. All this time, John McCourd sat quietly in the corner of Bouviard's kitchen.

When the crowd refused to leave, an argument ensued as to who was or wasn't an Orangeman. Fisticuffs broke out, a door was smashed and Mrs. Bouviard was knocked to the floor. Realizing he was outnumbered, Bouviard went for his gun, but one of the rowdies wrested it away from him and in the tussle it flew into the air and tumbled down the cellar stairs, landing at the bottom.

By this time, the crowd had moved outside but was still unruly and threatening. That's when Bouviard raced down to the cellar to retrieve his pistol; he tripped in coming up the stairs, causing the gun to bang against the stairs and discharge, hitting the innocent John McCourd full in the abdomen.

Bouviard ran to him and cradled him in his arms as McCourd whispered, "I'm shot. But I forgive you." Mrs. Bouviard plumped two pillows under him and covered him with a blanket. By the time the doctor arrived, McCourd had lapsed into semiconsciousness and could be heard praying softly as the life seeped out of him.

At the inquest, there were several eyewitness versions of the evening's events recorded. One witness claimed that it was Mrs. Bouviard who caused the misplaced shot to discharge from the gun when she tried to wrestle it from her husband's hands. But no proof of that version was ever uncovered, and although she had shouted out that night that it was indeed her fault that McCourd was dead, when it came time to tell her story under oath, it had changed considerably.

The bottom line was that once all the witnesses had given their testimony, Bouviard was discharged from custody and the charges against him were dropped. The final ruling read:

> That the said John McCourd came to his death between the hours of two and three o'clock on the morning of July 26, 1874, from bleeding occasioned by a gun shot wound made by a gun in the hands of William Bouviard. And that the shooting was accidental. And the jury thinks the case was aggravated by the circumstances that brought a disorderly crowd to his house. And that he was guilty of gross carelessness in the use of his gun.

In spite of that finding, Bouviard got off scot-free. All of this leaves us to wonder what happened to James McCourd's young child, the one he was working so hard to support and that was now an orphan.

WOBURN'S URBAN LEGEND

E very city and town can lay claim to their very own urban legend, and Woburn is no exception. Woburn's urban legend originates from a family tale told to Anna Lascurian and Anita Stratos as children. The tale tells of a haunted house on Everett Street.

The house at 17 Everett Street no longer exists because it was too dangerous to be allowed to coexist alongside perfectly respectable houses that had the decency to keep their spooky secrets to themselves; this bold dwelling sent tenants packing after only a few days.

I became aware of this "Woburn-ville Horror" about a year ago when an e-mail from Anna Lascurian that originated in New Jersey was forwarded to me in the hopes that I could help her uncover information that would validate a legend repeated at family gatherings—a legend that has plagued their family for three generations.

It was Anita who filled me in on the details and described "a rather strange house that existed in Woburn sometime in the 1930s," and Anita's tale goes something like this.

The house at 17 Everett Street was once a large and beautiful home built by a doctor at the end of the nineteenth century. When the doctor died, his wife vacated the house immediately and rented it out in hopes of bringing in some revenue. But in spite of the fact that she arrived in person each month to collect the rent, she "refused to cross the doorway" and would routinely wait outside till the tenant handed her the rent money.

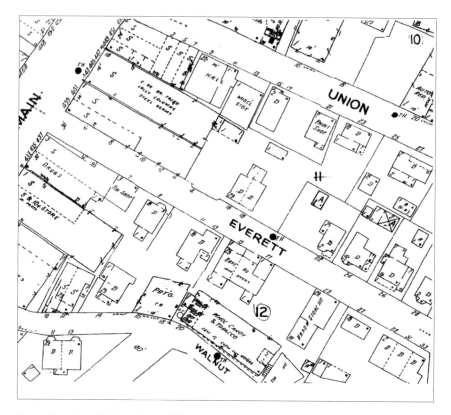

Footprint of the "Urban Legend" house at 17 Everett Street as it appeared on the 1926 Sanborn map, appropriately labeled "No Owner."

As it turned out, the turnover in tenants was frequent and no one lasted longer than nine months. At many times, the house went unoccupied until a tenant could be found who was unaware of its reputation. During those interludes, neighborhood boys would sneak inside to play, only to be frightened away by ghostly happenings. One young man was so desperate to escape one of these spectral beings that he jumped from a second-floor window, breaking his leg in the process.

But Harry (Aristides) and Foutoula Paris were "stubborn disbelievers" and refused to believe the ghost stories. They were recently married and determined to enjoy the large house and low rent and not look a gift horse in the mouth. In fact, they remained in the house for two or three years, rationalizing the unexplained and denying the possibility that ghosts existed.

When Harry and Foutoula were moving in, the moving men had a dog with them that refused to enter the house. When he was finally coaxed just inside the door, his hackles rose in alarm, and he ran as if being pursued by the devil, yipping all the way, never to be seen again.

If that wasn't enough, that first night in their new home was interrupted when both sat bolt upright in bed at exactly the same moment. When they compared stories, both told of the same nightmare, which featured a bony-fingered hand grasping at their necks and refusing to let go.

The following morning Foutoula found all the pictures that she'd hung so carefully the day before turned and facing the wall. But most frightening of all was that their son, only nine months old at the time, would often sit upright in his crib and stare off into space, telling an unseen entity, "Shhhhhh." Overnight guests heard more than bumps in the night. Often they would wake sleepy-eyed and ask why Harry and Foutoula allowed people to make all that noise on the attic steps all night.

Once, when Foutoula was relaxing in the living room, she heard someone enter the basement and assumed it was the meter reader. But when she didn't hear him leave, she went to investigate.

"When she reached the bottom of the stairs," Anita reports, "she felt all the energy drain from her and her knees turned to jelly and she collapsed onto her knees. She felt a sense of dread come over her, a sense of evil." As soon as she composed herself, she clawed her way back up the stairs as if struggling to get free of some ghostly grasp. When she reached the top of the stairs, she discovered her fingers were bleeding.

That frightening episode was enough to prompt Foutoula to call a priest to bless the house. But after only a few minutes across the threshold, he turned to her and said, "Move away from here."

Still unconvinced, it took one final episode to make believers of the Parises. As they sat eating dinner one night, a man suddenly appeared out of nowhere, passed through the kitchen door, strode across the room, passed through the cellar door and thumped down to the stairs without a word.

That was it for Harry and Foutoula. They gathered up their two sons and ran from 17 Everett Street, leaving Harry's week's pay on the kitchen table and never looking back.

Harry and Foutoula had almost lost something more valuable than a week's pay though. Their seemingly perfect marriage had begun to show signs of strain. They began to argue over inconsequential matters. But, according to relatives, once they moved out of 17 Everett Street, they picked up their perfect marriage where they left off and got along just fine.

Rumor has it that the doctor and original owner of the house had performed some ghoulish experiments on some unfortunate souls he believed wouldn't be missed, and buried them in the basement. When word leaked to police, they launched an investigation, which ended with them taking the house at 17 Everett Street apart "brick by brick." But they found nothing and no record was kept of any investigation.

In my research, I did uncover an Aristides (Harry) and Foutoula Paris listed in the city directory as living at 17 Everett Street in 1932. Their son Arthur was the husband to Barbara Haynes and father to Florence, Katherine and Harry Paras and died in 1984. He is buried at Woodbrook Cemetery and, with him, Woburn's urban legend of the house at 17 Everett Street.

IF WALLS COULD TALK, CIRCA 1900

E very house has a story to tell. But, one wonders, if a house changes its appearance to the point that it no longer resembles the original structure, do its walls still ring with the stories of its past?

That question haunted me recently as I was recording the history of a house on Main Street. The house, originally at 842 Main Street, seemed to have disappeared off the map. At first, I assumed it was one more of the city's architectural treasures that became victim to the wrecking ball, but just to be sure, I called someone who knew the history of that house firsthand.

After a brief conversation with a friend of one of its early occupants, I was able to ascertain that the house was still there but had morphed so drastically that it was hardly recognizable. In fact, what was once 842 Main over time became 846 Main and only vaguely resembled the original, elegant structure that stood there in the late 1800s. But considering there were still vestiges of that stately home lingering on that spot, I decided to record some of the more interesting events that occurred there.

At the turn of the twentieth century, the pie-shaped piece of land— bordered by Main and Elm Streets and Newbridge Road, where 842 Main Street once stood—was graced with homes and gardens that made them country estates worthy of note. And in the case of 842 Main Street, summer transformed it into a refuge for working women from sixteen Massachusetts cities and towns who otherwise could not afford a vacation in the country.

The Hoag Family, shown with Elinor in the driver's seat, posing for a family photo, circa 1900. *Courtesy of Elinor Hoag.*

The organization sponsoring the program was called the International Sunshine Society, and thanks to the generosity of Mr. and Mrs. John Benjamin Hoag, their gracious home at 842 Main Street became a refuge to countless working women throughout the early 1900s. But considering the character and commitment the Hoags made to their community, one would expect such generosity from them.

It was told to me that Mrs. Hoag built the house at 842 Main on her parents' property in the late 1800s when she was still Miss Martha Elizabeth Leslie, and then when she married in 1897, the newlyweds moved into the house. Both John and Elizabeth "Lizzie" Hoag were principals of Woburn schools—Mrs. Hoag was principal of the Wyman School and John Hoag was principal of the Cummings School as well as the Rumford and Linscott Schools later on in his career, so their commitment to the youth of the city was well established.

When the Hoags were asked to lend their home to the Malden branch of the International Sunshine Society, they readily agreed. After all, the house stood idle every summer while the Hoag family made their way to the lakes region of Center Sandwich, New Hampshire, for a season. And what better way to assure that their garden would be tended and their elegant home put to good use than to open it to such a worthy organization.

Mr. John B. Hoag riding his bike in front of his home at 842 Main Street as it looked in the early 1900s. *Courtesy of Elinor Hoag.*

In researching the history of the International Sunshine Society, I was intrigued by the fact that its founder, Cynthia Westover Alden, whose varied career was highlighted by her charity work, later became the editor of the women's department of the *New York Recorder* in 1897. But it wasn't until 1900 that she incorporated the International Sunshine Society, which she oversaw until she died in 1931.

By then the society had over five hundred branches in thirty-eight states and eight foreign countries. Its good works included helping disadvantaged children, working women and the blind. So it was that under Alden's tutelage that the Malden branch of the Sunshine Society was established in 1900 and, with the Hoags' help, the "Good Cheer Camp" in Woburn opened to more than one hundred young working women.

The camp garnered some publicity when it came to Woburn and the Hoags' home was described in a July 1901 *Boston Globe* article as "the jolliest sort of a sunshine vacation home for Massachusetts' girls with small means."

The house at 842 Main Street was described as set

> *back from the street* with a *shady grape arbor along one side and a great broad piazza with woodbine shading it, where there are hammocks and swings heaped with cushions. And out in the backyard there is such a sizable and varied vegetable garden that the camp mother has but to buy potatoes, the rest of the needful vegetables being picked from the grounds*

Mrs. Elizabeth Hoag sitting in the parlor of the Hoag Family home at 842 Main Street, Woburn, Massachusetts, circa 1900. *Courtesy of Elinor Hoag.*

fresh every day. It is just this home effect which prevents Good Cheer Camp from seeming in the least bit institutional.

With as many as thirty-four girls ages twelve and up in residence during each two-week period, the Good Cheer Camp buzzed with activity. And all that activity was overseen by the "camp mother," Mrs. Emory E. Bennett, who hosted a party once a week for the campers' friends and families from the city.

And, as the *Boston Globe* article explains, "'Ma,'" as the campers called Mrs. Bennett, "doesn't do all the cooking. Once a week slips are made out containing the names of every girl then at the camp, and they draw lots as to who shall get to cook the dinner. No one else than the chosen girl is allowed in the kitchen" and she "can appropriate anything in the pantry, vegetable garden and orchard to put together her menu."

The atmosphere created by the "camp mother" was a festive one that combined "a vacation in the country with the acquiring of some form of useful knowledge. There is a teacher of embroidery and one of basketry; and there is a piano, on which the girls not only bang out rag-time, but upon which they conscientiously practice five-finger exercises and scales."

There was also a daily paper put together by the Sunshine girls and bound in the camp colors of yellow and white and in which the ladies were encouraged to be creative in their content. To make for an even homier feel, each room of the house was given a name and over the front door hung a sign that read: "Our door is closed to Envy, Hate and Pride; But to a simple Friend it is ever opened wide."

But it is the following description used to summarize their experience that must ring through the vestiges of the old mansion at 842 Main Street:

> Good Cheer Camp is so much more meaningful than the average vacation home. It stands for the joyous courage of the commonplace. It is a simple country vacation place for the girl of small means, the girl who realizes that her path in life will probably be the middle one, where the demand for courage is the greatest since all the reward that can be legitimately expected must come from within.

If only the walls at 842 Main Street could talk, what stories they could tell.

SAME-SEX MARRIAGE, CIRCA 1878

When Sarah Maud Pollard arrived in Woburn, Massachusetts, about 1870, she had a secret. But her secret was hard to keep, especially from her co-workers at the Simonds Shoe Stock Factory. Even young boys in the Woburn neighborhood where she had taken refuge with relatives taunted her with the nickname "the Great Eastern," a reference to the huge Leviathan vessel that the Great Eastern Steamship Company used to lay the North Atlantic cable back in 1866.

Sarah Pollard was a big woman, to say the least. Not only was she big by female standards, she was big by male standards as well. And the fact that her voice bellowed in a deep baritone when she talked and that her upper lip showed signs of a mustache, through no fault of her own, called attention to her masculine side. But although speculation ran high, no one knew for sure until a news story was telegraphed to Woburn about a Samuel Pollard under arrest in Tuscarora, Nevada.

Sarah Pollard left Woburn about 1873 to go to work in a shoe shop in Stoneham, but when that didn't work out, she returned to her hometown of Binghampton, New York, where things went well for awhile. She started her own business in the "manufacture of shirts" and did quite well until she ran into some business reverses so severe that she lost all her property, left Binghampton and headed west.

The next time anyone made note of a Sarah Pollard was when she was sighted in Denver, Colorado, about 1875. According to comments made by people who came in contact with her in Denver, she was very hard to miss. News reports of the day describe a woman with distinctly mannish qualities arriving at a fair in Denver after traveling there by train.

The 1875 Beers Map that outlines the Pollard property where Sara Pollard stayed with relatives while working in Woburn.

Not only did Sarah Pollard make herself well-known in Denver in the few days she was there, she also left a lasting impression on her fellow travelers. As reported in the *Woburn Journal* on June 8, 1878, a woman thought to be Sarah Pollard formerly of Woburn, Massachusetts, arrived in Denver wearing a

> *felt hat of alpine shape, with a brown velvet band around the crown—*
> *the only trimming; a white stand-up collar encircled her throat. In her*
> *hand she carried a huge brown portmaneau* [suitcase]. *Her upper*
> *lip bore vestiges of a mustache. A whisper ran around* [among her
> fellow traveling companions], *'She looks more like a man than*
> *a woman.' To several onboard the train, the journey is to this day a*
> *horrible nightmare in which the chief figure is a gaunt, mannish woman,*

A gold mine in Tuscarora, Nevada, similar to the one worked by Sam/Sarah Pollard in 1877. *Courtesy of the Elko County Collection, Elko, Nevada.*

perpetually advocating and advancing the most radical sentiments in a hoarse, guttural voice.

Her experience in Denver must have been a turning point for Sarah, because by the time she arrived in Tuscarora, Nevada, a few weeks later, Sarah had morphed into Samuel. Tuscarora came late to the gold rush and when it finally did, it got off to a slow start, but that didn't stop it from becoming a rough-and-tumble mining town. Founded by a prospecting party that had set out from Austin, Texas, to find their fortune, by 1869 Tuscarora was beginning to attract a diverse and most interesting population.

First to arrive were the Chinese prospectors who, upon the completion of the Central Pacific Railroad, suddenly found themselves out of work. Soon after they arrived, they built a genuine Chinatown just inside Tuscarora town limits and so began a raucous era in Tuscarora that attracted adventurers from all over the world and became the perfect place for someone looking to start a new life—that fell in perfectly with Samuel M. Pollard's plans.

Later on, many reasons were given for Sarah's morphing into Samuel, but one thing was for sure, the people of Tuscarora knew only Samuel. News reports note that, "At Tuscarora she appeared in male attire," and took up placer mining like many of the men who had come before him to make their fortune.

Samuel had hardly settled into life in Tuscarora when he "captivated" the heart "of one of the belles of the town," a Miss Marancy Hughes. But Marancy's family was not as captivated with Samuel as she was. In fact, they opposed the match so completely that Samuel and Marancy finally eloped and got married in the county seat of Elko in September of 1877.

For six months, Samuel and Marancy lived what seemed to the casual observer a quiet, contented life in a neighboring town. Then suddenly Marancy appeared back among her family and friends in Tuscarora with the "startling assertion" that her "husband was a woman."

Her story, as told in the *Woburn Advertiser* on June 6, 1878, went somewhat like this:

> *On the bridal night the woman-husband explained that she had adopted male garments to escape arrest for a crime committed in another state, that she had determined to marry to add to the success of her disguise, and she further remarked to her little wife that if she betrayed her secret she would beat her to death. For six months, the maiden wife states she has lived in fear of her woman husband, who frequently beat and abused her in every way. The imposter was described as large and masculine looking, but the wife says that she is as perfectly formed a woman as ever lived and wore an under vest of stout cloth tightly laced across the bust to conceal the outlines of her form.*

Many who knew Samuel well didn't believe he could be abusive to anyone, let alone someone he claimed to love, but in any case Marancy stuck to her claim to have "escaped" from Samuel. She said that when he went off on a business trip and left her behind, she took that opportunity to make good her escape.

Now free from his grasp, Marancy became captive to the center of a firestorm of controversy that spread all the way to California and back east as well. She was compelled to tell her tale over and over again, and each time she did, things didn't seem as cut and dry as Marancy had once claimed. As a result, the only charge that could be made against Samuel was that he lied about being a man on his marriage license.

The *Woburn Advertiser* reported that "Samuel, or Sarah, as the case may be, was arrested after his arrival home on a charge of perjury and the case was continued." The next day, the *Woburn Journal* scooped the *Advertiser* with this: "Sarah has been arrested on a charge of perjury and the injured wife writes to the local paper to know if there is not some law by which she can be punished for the imposition she had practiced."

In the swirl of a news frenzy, many confusing versions of the story appeared in local papers in Nevada, Arizona and California. On one website (http://nvghosttowns.topcities.com/pastpro/tuscaror.htm) that catalogues the history of Nevada ghost towns, the Pollard-Hughes story was recorded in one short paragraph along with the history of Tuscarora, Nevada, today a genuine ghost town.

> *An incident in 1879* [according to Woburn newspaper reports, the incident occurred in 1878] *brought about great interest because of its bizarre nature. A local woman was married but shortly afterward left her husband because she found that he was actually female. The husband, known as Sam Pollard, was believed to be male by his fellow miners. Pollard, whose real name turned out to be Sarah, had devised the scheme to protect her* [Hughes] *from her father.*

On June 13, 1878, the *Woburn Advertiser* followed up with this stunning conclusion: "The latest from the Pollard-Hughes affair of Tuscarora, Nevada is that when Pollard came into court to be tried for perjury, the Hughes girl, whom Sarah or Samuel Pollard married, fell to weeping and finally embraced her 'husband' and they all went out of court together."

Whether Samuel and Marancy lived happily ever after was not reported. But I have been in touch with the archivist at the University of Nevada library to request more information from local Nevada newspapers to see if there is more to the story. So far I have not received a reply.

I did find out through my own research that Samuel went on to become a featured speaker throughout the Southwest, appearing dressed as half man–half woman and telling his story to all who would listen. Samuel Pollard, or Sarah if you prefer, continued living in and around Tuscarora, Nevada, and was well accepted by his neighbors, which no doubt is a tribute to his character.

With the tumult being created presently by the battle over same-sex marriage, it seems that once again history has something to teach us. It is also rather startling that Sarah/Samuel Pollard could gain acceptance the wilds of a Nevada ghost town in 1878, while 126 years later we here in the so-called liberal Northeast continue to divide ourselves into culture camps of no consequence.

SUICIDAL PARROTS AND GYPSY ROYALTY

Not all of Woburn's history tells of tragedy and courageous acts of patriotism. Sometimes its hidden history reveals itself to be less solemn, although somewhat touching. But in the end, those little-known stories do indeed comprise the heretofore-solemn history of Woburn as well as bring a smile to your face. So, let me begin with the story of the suicidal parrot.

It all began when David Katcoff, caretaker of the Jewish cemeteries on Washington Street near the Winchester line, returned home one day in March of 1914 to discover his pet parrot was among the missing.

Katcoff had left his caretaker home/office, and his beloved pet of thirteen years, in the care of an employee named Charley, who was known to be somewhat unreliable from time to time due to his occasional bouts with demon rum. So when Katcoff noted that his pet parrot was not on his usual perch, he became suspicious.

That set him to questioning Charley. During his cross-examination, Katcoff noted that Charley was slurring his words and showing an unsteady gait and knew he was not going to get a straight story from Charley. So Katcoff made a quick search of the place for his longtime companion and much-loved pet.

Although he didn't immediately find his Polly, he did notice a collection of feathers strewn about on the floor, and that led to the discovery of his beloved parrot's fine-feathered corpse carelessly flung in a laundry basket.

At this point, Katcoff notified the police, and when they arrived and confronted Charley, he admitted to throttling the bird, so they placed him under arrest.

David Katcoff and his wife Jennie (date unknown). David was the caretaker of the Jewish cemetery in 1914 Woburn when his beloved parrot "committed suicide." *Courtesy of the Katcoff family.*

The next day, when Charley's case came before the court, Katcoff found a sympathetic ear in the presiding judge. It seems Judge Morton was also a proud parrot owner. In fact, when Katcoff explained to the judge that his parrot knew everyone in the neighborhood by name and would inform them of his whereabouts if he wasn't home, the judge was somewhat envious. It seems Judge Morton's parrot hadn't nearly the vocabulary that Katcoff's did.

The judge later noted that it was just that talent that led to the precocious parrot's demise. You see, that pugnacious parrot not only knew the neighbors' names, it knew Charley better than Charley did.

So well, indeed, that when Charley was in an obvious state of inebriation, the parrot would shout, "Charley's drunk again! Charley's drunk again!" loud enough to wake the dead. But this time Charley had just about had it with those verbal slurs on his character, and claimed that the parrot's parroting of that insulting yet accurate phrase over and over again caused him to lose his temper and off the pesky parrot.

That was also Charley's defense. Charley claimed that because the parrot chose to keep repeating "Charley's drunk again!" and ignore his pleas to cease and desist, he effectively caused his own demise by forcing Charley to act. In essence, Charley claimed, the parrot ultimately committed suicide by choosing to ignore him, and he pleaded innocent on the grounds that the parrot made him do it.

The judge disagreed, and while Katcoff stood nearby with his pet parrot's corpus delecti in a paper sack, the judge ordered Charley to spend a month of reflection at the Billerica House of Correction on a charge of public drunkenness, noting there was no law on the books against parrotcide. Judge Morton also declared that, "This was a parrot that talked too much."

Now we move on to a tale of intrigue, royalty, hidden treasure, greed and murderous threats. No, it's not about the city council. It's about a time when gypsies camped in Woburn and caused all manner of turmoil.

The year is 1917. The place is New Boston Street, where a band of gypsies set up camp and set in motion a chain of events that added some mystifying foreign intrigue to the otherwise dull lives of the local law and order establishment.

That the gypsies made camp on New Boston Street is not unusual for that era, but what were extraordinary were the events that followed. It all began when two gypsy tribes camped together and then clashed over the most common cause of unrest since the first man traded the meat of a dinosaur for a mastodon tusk—money.

It seems the camp's queen, Marcia Mock, had earlier made an alliance with the Johnson Tribe of Whitman, Massachusetts, through a marriage of sorts with the son of the Johnson Tribe leader, Steve Johnson. But things turned from bad to worse when, after a falling out, Steve Johnson asked for the return of the treasure he had given Queen Mock for safekeeping. Queen Mock responded by saying the equivalent of, "In your dreams Steve."

That sent Steve Johnson running for help to the one institution that was more likely a gypsy's enemy back then, although in this situation it was his only hope. Johnson showed up at the Woburn Police Station with a warrant secured by his lawyer for the arrest of Queen Marcia Mock, and he wanted it acted on before Mock made off with his loot.

The police responded by raiding Mock's camp and searching for the hidden treasure that they had no real expectation of finding. Hence they were stunned beyond all belief when they found bags full of gold and cash in excess of $10,000, a king's ransom back in 1917.

Of course, Queen Mock was not about to go silently into this good night. She, too, hired a lawyer, insisting the fortune was hers and not Steve

Johnson's. But Johnson's credibility was enhanced when he claimed there was another $3,500 dollars in large bills missing from the count and then produced a certificate of authenticity from the Rockland Trust Company showing that he had indeed withdrawn $5,900 in large bills in April of 1917. So the police once again raided the gypsy camp and found that exact amount in the predicted denominations hidden inside a newly sewn pillow, just as Johnson had foretold.

So tense was the situation between the two gypsy royal families that Woburn's Judge Johnson (no relation) held a court session late that same night in the police station because gypsy leader Johnson feared for his life as long as he was in possession of the much-sought-after treasure. He said the woman, meaning Queen Mock, "would stick a knife in herself and blame it on me" if given the chance.

At one point in the court proceedings, Queen Mock, anxious to secure her release so she could exact her revenge on Johnson, offered the court a bag full of gold necklaces in lieu of bail. But police were reluctant to keep such a tempting treasure on police premises. That's when Judge Johnson came forward and offered to make arrangements for the safekeeping of Queen Mock's unusual bond.

The judge then found in Johnson's favor and made arrangements for him to store his loot in the vault of the local bank until he could transfer it to a Boston bank the next morning. To show his appreciation to both police and the court, Steve Johnson presented everyone with boxes of premium cigars.

When the sun rose next morning, Woburn police sent Queen Mock and her royal pains in the court packing, admonishing them never to darken Woburn's door again. And they haven't—at least as far as I know.

Walnut Hill Community Club and the Great Depression, circa 1936

In a recent conversation with Woburn's Bernice (Bonnie) Flynn Shay, now of Tewksbury, I was told a fascinating story of how the neighbors in her tiny neighborhood pulled together to rescue an elderly widow from the degradation of poverty during the Great Depression of 1929. The neighborhood was the Walnut Hill section of the Woburn, now referred as the Newlands.

The Newlands is a neighborhood in East Woburn bordered by Wildwood Street, Mishawum Road and Beach Street, but back in 1936 when this particular story unfolded, there were only a few dirt roads and even fewer houses built on what had been the Walnut Hill Farm. In fact it was a brand-new neighborhood, and in order to make sure the residents got the necessary municipal improvements they needed, like water mains, sidewalks and street paving, they formed a group called the Walnut Hill Community Club.

Right about that time, Bonnie Flynn had graduated from high school and took on the duties as secretary for the club. As a result of her efforts, a detailed record of how the Walnut Hill Community Club rescued a frail widow living under deplorable conditions has been preserved, and the compelling story of Widow Lillian Mason can be told.

The story began when news spread through the Walnut Hill neighborhood in July of 1936 that Lillian's husband, John Mason, had died. That prompted many of the neighbors to stop by the Mason home to pay their respects to his widow. But what they found upon entering the deplorable shack on Hinston Street where John's widow was living

Walnut Hill Station, built in 1835, located south of Salem Street Bridge in the Walnut Hill section of Woburn. *Courtesy of the Fowle Collection.*

prompted the neighbors to take on the task of seeing to it that the widow be provided with suitable housing.

John and Lillian Mason's connection to Walnut Hill began when they had finally saved enough money to buy a piece of land on which to build their dream home. That's when they chose the Walnut Hill section of Woburn, also known as the Newlands. It was 1924, and with both in their mid-fifties, they believed it might be their last chance to have a place of their own where they could spend their final years in relative comfort. But it was not to be.

No sooner had they settled into what they thought would be a temporary campsite than John lost his job at one of the local tanneries. Lillian tried to help out by working at any job she could get, both nights and weekends, but things went from bad to worse when the Great Depression of 1929 hit full tilt.

By then, both John and Lillian were entering their sixties, and although John had found another job in Boston that he thought would carry him through the depression years, he was soon disappointed. As it turned out, his employer told him he was too old for the job and that they were hiring a younger man to fill his position. From then on, his hopes of ever being gainfully employed again were dashed, and with no family to turn to, he and Lillian were left completely on their own.

To make matters worse, the winter of 1935 was particularly harsh and with no heat in their drafty shack, John contracted pneumonia. A doctor was out of the question and although she did her best to nurse her husband back to health, Lillian was not up to the task and his condition worsened until he finally succumbed to his illness that following July.

Now Lillian found herself completely on her own. That is, until neighbors began to stop by to pay their respects. It seems the people of Walnut Hill actually cared about one another and seeing the lonely widow living under such deplorable conditions prompted a community effort so unparalleled that it soon became national news. Once the story broke, every newspaper and radio show in the country was reporting the story of the neighbors who cared enough to build a home for a destitute widow.

Not surprisingly, the effort began when Bonnie Flynn Shay's parents, Mr. and Mrs. Willis Flynn and Mr. and Mrs. Robert Soderholm, called a neighborhood conference. The result of that meeting was the decision to build widow Mason a house as a gift from the neighborhood. After all, what are neighbors for?

After that, the donations began pouring in. Present and past mayors made donations, along with the employees of the John Boole Company of Boston, where Mr. Mason had worked before being let go. The proceeds of whist parties and committee collections were added to the fund for a total of $154.95, which covered the expense of the lumber, doors, windows, cement and more that was necessary for construction.

In the final tally, when expenses were deducted from the proceeds, there was a balance of thirty-seven cents and only two unpaid bills remaining. The rest of the materials—which included plumbing supplies, paint, furniture and other materials used in the completion of the tiny but sturdy and well-heated bungalow—were all donated by the very generous neighbors of Walnut Hill.

Also, I would be remiss if I didn't mention that all labor was provided free of charge by the neighbors, and it should come as no surprise that Bonnie Shay's father, Willis Flynn, oversaw the entire project as chief architect, draftsman and mechanic.

By late September of 1936, the story had spread far and wide and the *Boston Post* conducted an interview with Mrs. Mason in which she explained her plight:

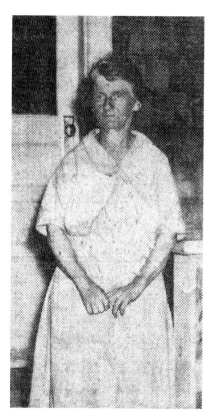

Left: The homeless widow, Lillian Mason, for whom the Walnut Hill Community Club built a cottage during the Great Depression.

Below: The cottage built by neighborhood volunteers for Widow Mason, who was found living in a drafty shack after her husband died in 1936.

We couldn't seem to get ahead. We were on welfare and then my husband died in July. The welfare people came and thought I wouldn't be able to stand the cold weather there and said they would have to fix it up. But my neighbors heard about it and they thought they could do something better than that. The Walnut Hill Community Club took charge and now my new home is almost finished.

Widow Mason moved into her two-room, twelve-by-eighteen-foot bungalow on Hinston Road, complete with electricity and running water, on Sunday, October 4, 1936. The occasion was well attended. The *Woburn Daily Times* reported that "neighbors stopped by all day bringing furniture, pots, dishes, curtains and rugs" and "Mrs. Robert Soderholm proudly accompanied Mrs. Mason into her new home."

On Tuesday, October 6, 1936, the *Boston Traveler* featured the headline "Victim of Depression Rewarded with Bungalow" and quoted Widow Mason as saying:

I just don't know how to thank everybody. I thought when my husband died last July leaving me alone in the world that life held nothing but hardship for me. Now I'm happy for the first time in years. I thought I'd never have my dream cottage. Well I guess I was wrong, for here it is, unless I'm dreaming. Life is good once more and the milk of human kindness hasn't evaporated yet.

THE LEGACY OF THE MERRIMAC CHEMICAL COMPANY, 1853–1929

From the day it opened in 1854 until it closed for good in 1929, there was hardly a workday that passed when someone wasn't injured or killed at Merrimac Chemical Works, once located in the northernmost corner of Woburn. But since it was considered Woburn's largest taxpayer, no one complained.

When Merrimac Chemical Works was founded by the triumvirate of Eaton, Hill & Chandler in 1854, its buildings covered a scant 3 acres, but by the time it changed hands in 1929, it had grown to more than ninety buildings that spread over 417 acres.

From 1854 to 1877, Woburn's Robert Eaton supervised daily operations, an arrangement that worked so well for investors that the company went public and changed to a stock company. That's when Robert Eaton hired a Mr. Howard of Boston to take on the daily operations. It was also at that point that the Eaton family profile was enhanced socially and they became an integral part of the cream of Woburn society. But the Eaton name was soon to go from envied socialite to community pariah as the nature of the business and its deleterious effects on the city and its citizenry become obvious.

One of those effects was the numerous fires that either wholly or partially destroyed the plant on more occasions than anyone cared to count. One fire in particular was remembered because of the bizarre death of the company's bookkeeper, Mr. Weeks.

Billed as one of the "most terrible fires Woburn had ever experienced," the 1879 fire raged uncontrolled when a fierce wind seemed to rise up from out of nowhere and threaten to destroy the entire complex of buildings. It was then that Mr. Weeks, fearing that the company books that he had labored over so diligently for years would be destroyed, raced back inside in an effort to rescue them.

But Mr. Weeks's feat of derring-do turned ugly when he toppled into a "tank of vitriol," more commonly known as sulfuric acid, and in spite of being rescued almost immediately, he died an agonizing death a short time later. Undeterred, Merrimac rebuilt, only to be consumed by fire and rebuilt time and time again.

The most comprehensive account of Merrimac Chemical's operation has to be the one a "reporter" for the *Woburn Journal* compiled in 1887. The report wasn't filed until January of 1888, but it's clear from his colorful narrative that his tour of what he called the "Works" took place on "a pleasant day in September."

As he reported:

> *Having long desired to visit the Works, I, with a friend, went one afternoon. Our road was mostly through woods. The trees wore their gayest livery, the birds were flying back and forth all the time singing their merriest songs, while some daring squirrel would run along the fence near our path occasionally stopping to look with his eyes full of mischief, at us, then running along again until at length he would disappear.*

But what greeted the reporter as he emerged from those woods onto the site of Merrimac Chemical Company was a landscape that can only be described as bleak. When he and his friend emerged from that pastoral copse, they were suddenly confronted with a collection of buildings with smokestacks spearing into the sky that belched smoke and chemical residue that had long discouraged wildlife from even visiting.

The first building they came upon was a round brick building, where Supervisor Howard kept his office and where they stopped to ask permission to examine the "Works." And Mr. Howard, being amenable to their request, began their tour at a building the reporter described as the size of a "skating rink."

At one end of the building, he noted a "double row of furnaces," where, he was informed, iron pyrite was constantly burning and belching gas through a large pipe that led the gas to a series of chambers made of lead so that they could withstand the effect of the corrosive end product that collected there.

An aerial view of Merrimac Chemical Company in North Woburn, which operated from 1853 to 1929.

Once in the chambers, "a chemical action of nitrous fumes and steam, which are forced into the chambers on to the sulphur gas" produces a weak version of sulfuric acid that is eventually boiled down. The end product was the most important product manufactured at the plant, a truly volatile form of sulphuric acid used in the manufacture of leather both locally and all over the country.

Some of that sulphuric acid was also used in making alum at the plant. Upon entering the building where the alum is manufactured, the reporter was told that this particular alum was made from clay imported from Ireland, which probably accounted for the fact that most of the employees were from the British provinces.

He went on to explain that, in spite of working with such volatile chemicals, those employees had little protection against accidents on site beyond the "rough woolen clothes" they wore year-round in hopes the heavy fabric will protect them. Some employees had even built houses around the chemical works and were so isolated they rarely ventured into town.

The tour continued in the building where the alum was made and the reporter described the process. It seems that not all of the sulphuric acid produced at the plant was exported. Some of it was used in the production of alum, a clay substance dissolved in sulphuric acid to form a green liquid. Strips of lead are then suspended in the liquid until a substance forms on them and slowly morphs into crystals that are moved into a drying room that blazes with heat through all four seasons. The crystals are then spread over shelves and the final product is packed into barrels and shipped all over the world.

The reporter then entered the "fire-stone building" where "flue stone" was burned. The process is similar to what occurred in the other buildings but part of this building was also used to manufacture sulphate of copper, used for industrial dying.

As some of the smaller buildings became part of the tour, a Mr. Melville took over and educated the reporter in the chemical processes that occurred there. Some of the buildings held kettles of salt and sulphuric acid that were constantly burned to produce a gas that is then passed through stoneware bottles. The bottles were filled with water that absorbed the gas and formed hydrochloric acid, sometimes referred to as muriatic acid.

More buildings loomed on the horizon and it appeared the tour would never end. Some smaller buildings were used for packing, but tin crystals were made in one was. There were still more buildings on the East Side of the railroad tracks, where rubber and varnish were made, while others were subcontracted out to private contractors who manufactured smaller amounts of chemicals for Merrimac Chemical.

Yet another building loomed ahead and this one was of particular interest as it was used in making silicate. The process included the heating of sand and soda ash, which produces a glassy-looking mass that was used in industrial bleaching.

But what struck the *Woburn Journal* reporter most was that although the "Works" covered 417 acres, included ninety buildings and was nationally known as the largest manufacturer of industrial chemicals in the country, they employed a mere sixty to seventy-five men in spite of the fact that it was a twenty-four-hour operation.

Judging from that statistic, it's obvious how Mr. Eaton managed to grow company profits at such a phenomenal rate. Like his counterparts of today, he managed to downsize to the point that company profits soared while workers were exposed to danger on a daily basis and the entire area was blighted.

In 1929, in a brilliant maneuver designed to assure that Monsanto Chemical Company would take over the number one spot as the leading manufacturer of industrial chemicals, Monsanto purchased the Merrimac Chemical Company for the single purpose of closing it down, thus eliminating their competition. Does any of this sound familiar?

And Merrimac Chemical remained closed, which was both good and bad. Good because it no longer spewed its pollution into the air, nor dumped its debris into pools that seeped into the water table. Bad because, whether intentional or not, it managed to create a wasteland that became a dumping ground for every industry that followed—that legacy continues today.

As I've said before, the more things change, the more they stay the same, and those who do not study history are condemned to repeat it. When weighing tax dollars against quality of life, let's hope we have learned a valuable lesson about keeping our covenant to make things better for the next generation.

WOBURN PARKWAY'S BURIED PAST

As daffodils begin to peek through the rustic greenery that defines the Woburn Parkway, the beauty of that oasis between Water Street and Woburn Parkway is accented by the colors of spring. But that strip of nature was not always a thing of beauty. There was a time when it was not only a blight upon the land but one that contributed to the pollution of Horn Pond, and beyond.

In fact, between 1827 and 1893, that entire area between Pleasant Street and Horn Pond was dominated by one of the largest tannery operations in Woburn. The tannery was owned by Stephen A Dow, the patriarch of one of the wealthiest families in the city and one that has a very colorful history.

The Dow Tannery belched smoke and soot from huge smokestacks that dominated a landscape surrounded by dozens of buildings that housed the machinery, materials and men needed to conduct the dirty business of tanning leather.

The main building was 180 feet by 40 feet, three stories high and included an attic where the process of currying leather took place, the final process in producing the finished product. Most of the other buildings were also three stories and had basements in which boilers belched and engines ground out the power to keep the machines running. There were also hundreds of tanning beds scattered around the property, some of which are still in evidence today.

For a time, the tanning of leather implemented natural products such as the bark of trees, plants, etc., but as Woburn became a leading leather producer in the United States and offered much-needed employment, owners began looking for faster and more efficient ways to tan leather. That led to the use of chemical techniques that employed chromium, lead, copper and zinc amalgams that turned the liquor pits into a source of contamination that impacted not only the citizens of Woburn but everyone downstream.

In spite of the fact that residents may have suspected that the very business that constituted the lifeblood of the city was fouling the air and water for generations to come, there was little proof and the issue went unaddressed until the Boston Water Board petitioned the Massachusetts Board of Health to issue a restraining order against the Stephen A. Dow Company for "discharging sewage into the Mystic Valley."

That restraining order was issued in November of 1889 but was soon quashed after a two-day work stoppage, which curiously occurred on Saturday and Sunday. By Monday, Stephen Dow's lawyer was successful in having the order withdrawn. As a result, when Monday rolled around, work at the tannery continued without missing a beat.

After all, when Abijah Thompson and Uriah Manning fist secured that bucolic fifteen acres from the Moses Tottingham estate in 1822, the thing that attracted them was the note about "water privileges" that went along with the property. "Water privileges" meant they could do whatever they wanted with the land and any refuse could be dumped into the stream that ran through it and then emptied into Horn Pond.

That also meant that the land was the perfect location for a tannery, and when Stephen Dow married Abijah Thompson's daughter, he was made a partner in the operation. Then, in 1861, when Thompson died, he inherited the tannery and kept it going full tilt.

As the tannery grew and the techniques of tanning became more volatile, the refuse dumped into Horn Pond became more than anyone bargained for. But according to a letter to the editor that appeared in the September 19, 1889 edition of the *Woburn City Press*, there were those who disagreed most vociferously with the opinions of the Boston Water Board.

The letter was signed, "A. Grant," who more than likely was Ward 3 Alderman Alexander Grant. Alderman Grant took issue with Medford's characterization of Woburn industry as the "so-called polluter" of the Mystic Pond water supply.

Grant instead pointed out that it was Woburn's natural and prior inheritance to use what is now the Mystic Valley Watershed as "drainage without compensation or damages." He bolstered his argument by stating

The Dow Chemical Company, once located where the Woburn Parkway is now and also runs parallel to Water Street to Ice House Park. *Courtesy of the Woburn National Bank Postcard Collection.*

that no legal remedy would prevent the pollution that dumps into the pond that came from every home, farm, piggery and hatchery along the Mystic and it's tributaries from reaching all the other cities and towns. In fact, Grant claimed that since Horn Pond's water is filtered through a sand bank before it makes its way southeast then why can't Medford do the same?

But Woburn's own sewage problems were reaching critical mass. In spite of Grant's seemingly logical argument, a letter entitled "A Plea for Horn Pond" that appeared in the *Woburn City Press* a month earlier was having a larger impact on the citizens of Woburn.

In fact, when the author of this letter wrote, "Would it not be wise to take the warning before it is too late, that your children and future generations may not point to you in condemnation, not only because you have allowed such beauty to be despoiled, but because you have allowed it to be polluted into a breeding place of miasma and disease?" her words hit a nerve with each and every citizen of Woburn who treasured the oasis of rest and reflection that Horn Pond had become.

Fate sometimes has a way of intervening, though, and so it was by fate that the Stephen A. Dow tannery came to an abrupt and ignominious end on April 29, 1893. That was the day the Dow tannery burst into flames and self-destructed as residents from the cities and towns around Woburn gathered on the surrounding high ground to watch.

The flames spread quickly. Employees at first tried to squelch the flames themselves but all to no avail. Years of saturation with oil, grease and other volatile chemicals throughout the complex made the fire impossible to extinguish. Even after a general alarm was sounded, the fire seemed to have a life of its own. Oil drums exploded and scattered shrapnel in every direction.

But as sparks flew skyward, residents of the area were hard-put to keep their own houses from burning down as well. Houses and shops as far away as Mr. Benjamin Ober's house on Canal Street and Russell's shop on Beacon Street were in danger, making it seem impossible to escape the flames. Days after, reports from as far away as Wakefield told of people finding burning cinders on their property.

Fortunately, in spite of the widespread damage, no one was seriously injured in the fire. It was not only Saturday, but it was also lunchtime and some 150 employees had exited the buildings to enjoy lunch in the late April sun. And the fear expressed that the fire had left so many unemployed didn't prove true as well.

In the end, the Stephen A. Dow tannery was so badly damaged that it was decided that they would not rebuild. Instead, the very next day they leased the Maxwell tannery in North Winchester and picked up where they left off, making sure their employees were not out of work even one day.

For years, the charred ruins of the Dow tannery continued to blight the neighborhood until it finally came under the control of the Metropolitan Parks Commission. The commission, with a great deal of urging from the city, demolished the tannery to make way for the new Woburn Parkway, which opened in August of 1914.

But from what I've been told by people who lived through that transformation, most of the tannery still exists under the few layers of soil that were used to cover the debris. All of this makes it appear to be a good location for an archaeological dig.

WOBURN'S OVALTINE CONNECTION

Did you know that Woburn has a connection to Ovaltine? Yes. You heard me. Ovaltine!

When Elinor Hoag died in 2003 at the age of 103, she was the only surviving child of John and Elizabeth (Leslie) Hoag of 842 Main Street in Woburn. And since Elinor never married nor had children, she left all her memories in the care of her dear friend Elizabeth Smith.

Among those memories are dozens of photos, documents and newspaper clippings dating back to the 1860s that catalog the Hoag and Leslie families of North Woburn as well as their ancestors and descendants. Fortunately for the Woburn Historical Commission, Elinor instructed Elizabeth to share that collection with the people of Woburn.

While poring over all the memorabilia, I came across a picture of Elinor Hoag's mother, Mrs. John B. (Leslie) Hoag, taken in the early part of the 1890s, standing in her garden at 842 Main Street. And there, looming behind her, is a building identified as the "Clark Coffee Mill." Along with the picture is an explanation as to why that building was so identified. The note reads:

> *Clark Coffee Mill: As I understand, the Mill faced Elm Street, and the Hoag and Clark backyards joined. Mr. Clark had customers who wanted a hot beverage for breakfast, but did not want the caffeine. So Mr. Clark developed a beverage called "cereal coffee" and was doing very well with it until someone from Battle Creek, MI, wrote to Mr. Clark and told him that they were feeding patients in a sanatorium and*

The Clark Phosi-Cereal Nervine coffee mill as it stands today still standing behind 21 Elm Street, Woburn, Massachusetts, circa 1890. *Courtesy of the author.*

wanted to know the contents of his "cereal coffee" in order to judge if it was safe to give to their patients.

Mr. Clark, wanting to be cooperative, answered the letter, and before he knew what was happening, "Battle Creek" produced "Ovaltine" and made a fortune and poor Mr. Clark went under.

As you can imagine, this appeared worth investigating, but my search for a mention of Clark Coffee Mill in Woburn's newspapers of the day was fruitless. So I turned in another direction and began researching the Clark name to see if something would pop up. And it did.

In an article that appeared in the *Woburn News* in December of 1894, a short sketch outlines the accomplishments of one John W. Clark, who it turns out is the very Clark who owned the coffee mill shown in the photo on this page. The reason for the news story was that John Clark had just been elected alderman of ward 6; although his biography was longer than the other aldermen and city councilmen elected that year, it held few clues to his involvement with Ovaltine.

First of all, you should understand that John Clarke's time in Woburn was brief and there is little information about him available in local resources. But I did learn that Clark settled in Woburn in 1892 with his wife and family at 21 Elm Street and opened his coffee mill in partnership with a Mr. Alden and with the intention of developing a new product called cereal coffee, the genesis of Ovaltine.

In fact, the factory that looms behind Mrs. Hoag in the photo is not called Clarke Coffee Mill. Instead, it was listed under the voluminous name of the Phosphi-Cereal Nervine Coffee factory. That sent me in anther direction as I attempted to make a connection between what was then called "cereal coffee" and Ovaltine, and it appears there is one.

As stated in the note, it was true that among the coffee drinkers of the day there were many who loved the taste of coffee but suffered adversely from the effects of caffeine. As a result of market forces, there were many attempts to produce a product that would satisfy their desire for a hot beverage in the morning without the side effects.

Also, since the main ingredient in cereal coffee is hops, it appears Clark and Alden chose their location for good reason. For three centuries, the Carter family, living along the Woburn and Wilmington town lines, made their living traveling along Elm Street on their way into the Boston with carts full of hops, which accounts for that area of Woburn being called "Hoptown."

But it appears that Clark and Alden were not the only entrepreneurs looking to get into the cereal coffee market. According to an article that appeared in a trade publication, the battle still rages. As recently as November of 2002, a British company "paid over $270 million to purchase the Ovaltine beverage line from Novartis AG, a Swiss conglomerate."

Which brings us to the eternal question: What exactly is Ovaltine? According to one source, "In the late nineteenth century, Swiss chemist George Wander invented a cheap process to harvest malt extract, a syrup derived from malted barley that's commonly used by beer brewers." But Wander's aim was more compassionate than Clark and Alden's. His hope was that "once fortified with goodies like vitamin D and phosphorous," his drink would someday win the world's battle against malnutrition.

Then, in the early 1900s, which was a time of greed much like today, it appears that Wander's son had a more marketable idea, one to create a product call "Ovomaltine." By adding ingredients like sugar, whey and beet extract to his father's creation, he marketed it as an energy booster. In 1909, it was exported to Britain and renamed Ovaltine.

In the 1930s, Britain saturated the U.S. market with Ovaltine promotions like the "Ovaltinies," which became so popular they had their own radio show until they were unmasked by Ralphie, the main character from the classic movie *A Christmas Story*. When he finally decoded their hidden message, it read: "Be sure to drink your Ovaltine!" To which Ralphie replied: "Ovaltine? A crummy commercial? Son of a -----!" But check it out for yourself; it's worth a good laugh.

So it appears that Clark and Alden were among thousands of others who were duped into investing in a market to nowhere while more powerful financial forces and robber barons did what they did best—robbed every one of their dreams. In fact, true to their legacy, Ovaltine once again packed a punch. In 2001, they closed their plant in the United Kingdom and put 245 people out on the street, a legacy worth remembering.

But getting back to the demise of John W. Clark's coffee mill (or, more appropriately, the Phosphi-Cereal Nervine Coffee factory), Clark did not fare well. And it would not take much to convince me that Battle Creek had something to do with the failure of his business, although I can't offer any direct proof.

It does appear, though, that success was not in the stars for John W. Clark. According to his obituary that appeared in the *Woburn Journal* of July 20, 1906, Clark met an untimely death at age fifty-five when he succumbed to injuries received when his new business, a patent leather factory also in North Woburn, burned to the ground on July 18, 1906.

If it's any comfort to John W. Clark, Ovaltine never took off in my house. In fact, I recently threw out a jar that had been sitting in my kitchen cabinet virtually untouched since 1979. In the prophetic words of my children when I tried to pass it off on them as cocoa: "Yuck."

Woburn's "Ya-Ya" Sisterhood

The "Ya-Ya Sisterhood" has nothing on the Robins. In fact, their friendship has endured more than seventy years of life's ups and downs. Yet, in spite of the vagaries of fate, their round robin letter project has defied a major mail strike in New York City and a devastating tornado in Tennessee.

The seven Robins—Sis Dobbins Shanahan, Jeannette Hoff West, Bonnie Flynn Shay, Margaret Dobbins Balch, Libby Langill Baldwin, Lillian White Kean and Irene Fagner Benn—have not only managed to keep in touch through the years via their round robin letter, but they have also chronicled life in the United States over the last half-century.

It all began at the United Methodist Church Sunday school in Woburn, where the Robins, with the exception of Jeannette, met for the first time. It was there that they came to know Elsie West, a woman who had such a positive influence on their lives that they wanted to keep that bond of friendship alive as a way of honoring her.

When Elsie West passed away on January 30, 1953, they made a group donation to her favorite charity, the Hospital Aide Society at the Choate Hospital. In the process of acknowledging their donation, Ruth Langill, the director of nurses at the Choate and sister of one of the Robins, suggested that the thank-you note be passed from one to the other until the whole group was included. They not only followed that advice, they took it one step further and began a round robin letter that has survived for over fifty years.

The Robins' letter has always started with Sis Shanahan in Woburn. She puts together the first page and passes it along to the next person,

The Robins on Plum Island. Left to right: Irene Fagner Benn, Libby Langill Baldwin, Sis Dobbins Shanahan, Lillian White Kean and Bonnie Flynn Shay, 1937. *Courtesy of the Robins.*

who adds some news and then passes that along until all seven Robins have contributed to the missive. It then makes its way back to Sis and she keeps guard over the collection for everyone.

"I pull off the parts of the letter that have gone 'round to everyone," Sis explains, "but it has to go through all seven of us before I do that. When it comes back, I keep the file. Recently, Bonnie and I got together and put everything in archival sheets to assure that all the letter would be preserved for anyone who might want to read them."

The mail flow between the Robins was interrupted on only two occasions. One occurred during a mail strike in New York City, as Sis explains, "We lost one letter, but we never lose the whole thing because once they have made the rounds of all the Robins I put them aside and start a new one. That time we lost whatever was in the mail and the chain was broken for two years until I started it up again in October of 1968."

When Sis started the Robin "flying again," she changed the order, explaining that she had found an even older letter sent by one of the Robins to the *Breakfast in Hollywood Radio Program* in 1947. In her letter, the Robin nominated Elsie West as Good Neighbor of the Week and the letter was signed, "The Friendship Circle." It was only a few years later that "The Friendship Circle" morphed into the Robins.

The other time a letter was lost was when a tornado hit the post office in Jackson, Tennessee, where Robin Libby Langill Baldwin lived. As

Tewksbury Robin Bonnie Shay explains, "Libby was in a nursing home there and her son would read the letter to her and she would write a paragraph and then he'd mail it for her. This time he mailed it the same weekend a tornado hit the local post office and our letter disappeared. But we keep hoping someone will find it like a message in a bottle."

After restarting the letter again in 1968, the order continued so that it left Woburn and made its way to Jeannette West. But that changed a few years ago when, in spite of being the youngest Robin, Jeannette was the first to pass away after a long bout with Alzheimer's. The Robins sent a rose bush to her husband Stan as a way of keeping her memory alive. Stan planted the rose bush and put a sign on it that read: Robin's Rose.

So dear was that tribute to Jeannette that when Stan moved recently, he took it with him and replanted it at his new home in Ogunquit, Maine. He then offered to take Jeannette's place in the round robin letter and thereby became the first male Robin. But, as Bonnie explains, "Unfortunately we only have three men left in the group, but when time comes that they are needed at least one, Bob Kean, is ready to get involved."

Once the letter makes its way to Maine and Stan West, it comes back to Bonnie in Tewksbury, who then sends it on to Sis's sister, Margaret Balch, in California. From there, Margaret adds her news and then sends it, until recently, on to Libby Baldwin in Tennessee and then to Lillian Kean in Virginia, who mails it to Irene Fagner Benn in Pennsylvania. Once it makes its rounds, it comes back to Sis in Woburn to become part of the Robin collection.

But the ravages of time have begun to take their toll on the Robins. Bonnie explains:

> A year ago I flew out to Tennessee and spent a week with Fran and Libby Baldwin's son and his wife. I spent time visiting Libby everyday in the nursing home where she is suffering from dementia and I kept a log of what went on. In her lucid moments Libby and I reminisced about our lives and sang some of the crazy old songs and parodies we knew. I even had her playing cribbage. In fact, we played all afternoon. But the next day I tried again and she said she didn't know how to play that game. When I came home, I sent the log I'd written to everyone, and it was like they had a visit with her too.

All the Robins went to Woburn High, four graduated with the class of 1936, and one each from the classes of 1933, 1934 and 1935. From

The Robins. *Left to right:* Sis, Jeannette, Mary, Bonnie, Libby and Lillian with spouses in 1981. *Courtesy of the Robins.*

time to time, they would visit one another and, as Bonnie wrote in recent article she sent to *Reminisce Magazine*, "we would share our joys and sorrows, getting together as career girls or at each other's wedding or to celebrate the birth of our children all of whom called us all 'auntie.'"

One visit made an impression on all the Robins. On a group visit to their Connecticut Robin a while back, "we walked the beach collecting colored glass" for one of the group to make what she called "romance candles." But as a joke, the Robins tossed in a few unexpected items like "an old shoelace, some chicken bones, pine needles, a broken comb, etc." The following Christmas, that Connecticut Robin presented the group with a special candle decorated with the beach junk they had thrown in her bag.

As Sis explains, "It's a personal history. Sometimes someone might mention the weather but it's mostly family stories and when I write my portion of it I bring them up to date on what is going on in the church."

Bonnie doesn't think the next generation in each family will carry on the tradition in spite of the fact that the Robins were known as "auntie" to all the children and their offspring. "I don't think anyone will carry on our Round Robin letter. I think its time has come and gone and I can't imagine they will continue it, but if they save it I'll be happy."

As Sis put it, "Time is now measured by how long the letter takes to make the rounds of all the Robins. There is no particular time frame, but we've actually done better the last few years keeping it going. But when that letter arrives, you drop everything, because it's like a gathering of your closest friends."

So here's to the Robins: Sis Dobbins Shanahan of Woburn, Massachusetts; Jeanette Hoff West, deceased, (husband Stan [Tunny] keeps the letter going from Maine); Bonnie Flynn Shay of Tewksbury, Massachusetts; Margaret Dobbins Balch of California; Libby Langill Baldwin, deceased, of Tennessee; Lillian White Kean of Virginia; and Irene Fagner Benn of Pennsylvania. May their letters continue winging their way across America for many years to come.

Aurora Village: A Grand Scheme

In the 1860s, the women's suffrage movement was picking up steam. Up to that point, everyone accepted the fact that Homestead laws were tilted in favor of men leaving women without inheritance rights and often evicted from their homes upon the death of their husbands. In 1871, Anna Cabot Lodge, the mother of Henry Cabot Lodge, came up with the idea of the Boston Co-Op Building Company as a way to help working women own their own homes. From that idea sprouted the "Women's Economical Garden Homestead League," organized to "establish industrial homestead settlements, in or near the City of Boston, exclusively for women."

One newspaper called it a "scheme" to elevate women to man's equal, and many men felt that women should never be on a par with men. It was true that the bill defied tradition by allowing women to hold up to $200,000 in nontaxable property and when a woman named Aurora H.C. Phelps actually took advantage of the bill to purchase sixty acres of land with the intent of chartering a Women's Economical Garden Homestead League in Woburn, the power it afforded her made for hard feelings.

In July of 1871, Mrs. Aurora H.C. Phelps began offering subscriptions to investors looking to finance her "scheme," and her determination was the start of a long battle between Aurora Phelps and her so-called investors. In the beginning there was a flood of donations that helped get the Woburn Homestead off the ground. Most invested because they believed her intentions were honorable, although as time went on many lost confidence in her ability to make a success of her venture.

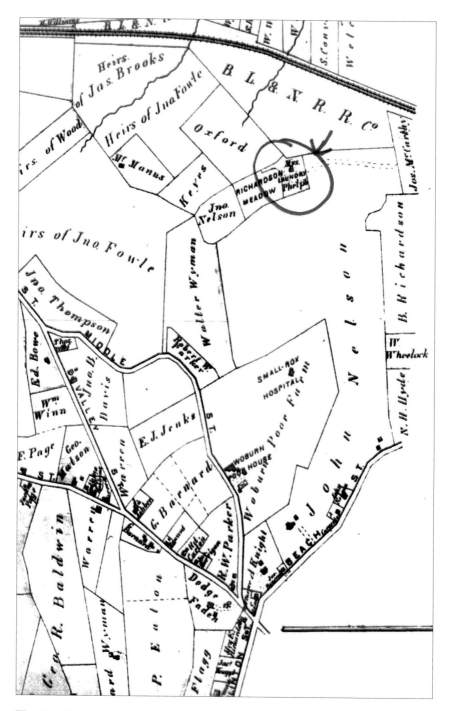

The 1875 Hopkins map, showing Aurora Village and its proximity to the BL&NRR, the Poor Farm and the Small Pox Hospital.

Finally, in September of 1873, ground was broken on that sixty-acre plot of land belonging to John Nelson that lay between what was then Beech Street and the Boston and Lowell Railroad in East Woburn. It was also not far from the Woburn Poor Farm and the Small Pox Hospital. One Boston newspaper described the location as being "in the heart of the forest of Woburn and 1 mile from any settlement" with only a cart path to the BL&NRR watering station. Today that area is a well-developed neighborhood between Beech Street, Middle Street and Atwood Avenue, stretching all the way to where Olympia Avenue and Wildwood Street intersect.

The plan was to establish a village that would eventually be owned exclusively by women in perpetuity. In fact, if any part of it was sold, it had to be sold to a woman. The village, which became known locally as Aurora Village, would have an industrial and domestic school on site, and some of its sixty acres would be set aside for gardening and fruit-raising. But what would drive the industrial engine that would keep Aurora Village economically viable would be a large scale laundry where the women would work and live until their houses were built.

The following month, the plan started to come together. An October 18, 1873 article in the *Woburn Journal* reported that when one of its reporters visited the site, he found that the cellar for the laundry had been dug and was "ready for building." A few days later, the *Woburn Advertiser* was present for the raising of the frame of the laundry that came to be christened as Bethesda Laundry, a biblical term for a "House of Mercy." Also, as local tradition dictated, neighbors came from all around to help in the raising of the laundry's walls.

It was a day of celebration, and when everything was ready, Aurora Phelps gave a short address, reminding an audience that didn't need reminding that the nature of her endeavor was a "philanthropic enterprise in which she engaged for the purpose of assisting the poorer classes." When Aurora finished her speech, Dr. Young, pastor of the First Baptist Church, offered a prayer and the "raising of the walls commenced." The building was sixty feet by twenty-five feet and two stories high with a full basement.

Once its walls were in place, Aurora took center stage and broke a bottle of water on its walls to officially christen it "Bethesda." She then invited everyone to partake of the refreshments that had been prepared for the occasion. To the unpracticed eye, it appeared that everything had gone off swimmingly, but it was the first of many slights to her benefactors and the beginning of the end of their support.

One slight was hinted at in the *Boston Daily Advertiser*, but as it turned out, it was a big one. It appears that one of the more prominent female reformers had been invited to speak at the raising of the Bethesda Laundry, but Aurora Phelps not only commanded the stage, she saw to it that Miss Jennie Collins and some of her well-known supporters didn't get to speak at all. Needless to say, in spite of their graciousness in not making a scene, the slight did not go unnoticed.

By December of 1873, the "House of Mercy" was anything but. According to a news story that appeared in the *Woburn Advertiser* the day after Christmas, there was little joy in what they termed the "incipient Aurora Village." It appears things were not going as planned but they were still rooting for Phelps. But her problem was a big one. It appears that the incipient village was in the hands of the sheriff and several attachments had been placed on its assets.

One lien was from a Mr. Jacob Whitcher for lumber and another from the Boston and Lowell Railroad for the transportation and delivery of said lumber, not to mention the numerous liens placed on Bethesda Laundry by all the carpenters that had worked so hard to construct the building. But Aurora still had her supporters and many were rooting for her to "extricate herself from her present unpleasantness and carry out her enterprise."

Unfortunately, by the summer of 1875, not only had local newspapers given up on any chance of success for the Woburn Women's Economical Garden Homestead League, but so had many of her affluent supporters. As the summer of 1875 rolled in, it appeared that, once again, Aurora Phelps was on her own, but this time she had more than a hundred women and children depending on her.

One headline in the July 1, 1875 *Woburn Advertiser* blared, "GRAND UPRISING OF THE AMAZONS," and that news story set the tone for what was to come. And although the headline may have been a little over the top, there was some justification for being disturbed by an incident at Aurora Village that was handled so badly by Phelps that it sparked a kind of rebellion.

Not only was Phelps embroiled in a legal struggle over the title to Aurora Village, things had become violent. It seems the neighbors were not too thrilled with Aurora Village's occupants and had attempted to force her out by setting fire to the Bethesda Laundry, the building where all the women and children lived and worked. Phelps became so enraged at these incidents that she was now armed to repel any invasion of her "sacred soil" and had fortified herself inside the Bethesda Laundry.

Aurora Village:
Uprising of
the Amazons

The tension at Aurora Village was building to a fever pitch, and it didn't help that the "Amazons" decided they needed more powerful weapons to defend themselves. Those weapons arrived on a sultry Monday evening in June of 1875. That's when Hart & Company express tried to deliver a large wooden box to the village. Aurora ratcheted up the tension by not only refusing to pay the expressman the delivery fee but also approaching him with three pistols strapped to her waist and ordering him to put down the box and leave. But the expressman was not intimidated and after an hour-long confrontation, he loaded the box back onto his wagon and returned to the train depot.

The women of the village pleaded with Aurora to pay the fee so they could have the weapons they needed to defend themselves, and she finally gave in. Upon arriving at the depot, she agreed to pay the $1.50 delivery fee if they would deliver it again. But when Hart & Company arrived a second time, the expressman told her there was now an extra fee of $0.25 for having to make a separate trip. This did not go over well with Aurora, and she drew one of her pistols, "pointed it at his head and ordered him to leave the box and go." Needless to say he did, and then made his way straight to the police to report the incident.

As if things weren't bad enough, Hart & Company express also notified the Woburn selectmen that the box had come from the state arsenal in Framingham and was filled with muskets—this bit of information got their attention. They took action immediately and sent a delegation to General Cunningham at the state arsenal to ask permission to remove the weapons from Aurora Village, and he agreed.

A teamster wagon similar to the one used by Hart & Company Express. *Courtesy of Fowle Collection.*

The following Friday afternoon, on July 2, 1875, a state deputy, accompanied by Woburn's Police Chief Mann and two of his officers, arrived at Aurora Village to confiscate the weapons, but Phelps was nowhere in sight. After much argument, they broke down the door, entered the laundry and ordered the woman in charge to produce the box of muskets. She answered that they were locked in Aurora Phelps's room and she couldn't get them until she came home.

What the women didn't count on was that the officers had a warrant, and they broke down the door to Aurora Phelps's bedroom and confiscated four loaded muskets and a box of "slugs." While there, they also noted that Phelps and the women and children in her charge had good reason to arm themselves. Upon inspection, they saw for themselves that Aurora Village was indeed under attack. There was evidence of fire damage in two locations, one around the door that, if it had not been extinguished in time, would have trapped them inside and made it impossible for them to escape.

In a letter to the *Boston Herald*, Aurora explained that when she "proposed to bring in some Irish children," a group of Woburn's prominent citizens objected. They claimed, "They would be damned if they would have a colony of Irish brats in their midst and would burn the place down before they would endure it." And the evidence showed, they did at least try to follow through with their threat.

It also appears from an article in the *Woburn Advertiser* that Aurora was physically not up to the challenge she had taken on. When some of her friends visited her at Bethesda Laundry on Wednesday, July 14, 1875, they found her "extremely ill." She was seized with spasms, and when the doctor came, he pronounced that her symptoms were similar to those produced by arsenic. Her friends then reported that the doctor analyzed the tonic she had taken and said that it did indeed contain arsenic.

All of this was a profound mystery to her friends, who claimed that "her recovery is said to be doubtful." But Aurora Phelps was not ready to give up the ghost and was soon back on her feet, creating havoc in no time. Her battle with John Nelson, the man who had sold her the land, ignited once again, and, as the *Woburn Advertiser* wrote, "The fair denizen of Bethesda Laundry is, we fear, in a state of chronic fractiousness."

The straw that broke the camel's back came in late July of 1875 when Nelson, in an attempt to secure his claim, began making use of his land by allowing a man named Tuttle to mow a field of tall grass to use as hay feed on his farm. But when Tuttle arrived to begin mowing, he found himself looking down the barrel of a gun aimed at him by one of Aurora's bodyguards. When Tuttle reported the incident to John Nelson, Nelson confronted Aurora's army and stood his ground.

Under his direction, Tuttle was allowed to mow the grass and rake it into hay piles that he planned to come back for the next day. But once again, Aurora had other ideas. In the dark of night, she and her army crept onto the field and, as a local newspaper described it, the hay sprouted wings and flew "where no man listeth." When Tuttle returned the following morning to resume his operation and found that his hay had been stolen, he reported it immediately to Nelson. But since it was raining quite hard, Tuttle and Nelson decided on another plan of attack.

The following day, on Saturday, July 24, 1875, Nelson returned with his own posse, and he meant business. He brought with him the chief of police, two reporters from local newspapers and dozens of workmen intent on securing their harvested hay. They advanced upon Bethesda Laundry with great purpose and when Aurora and her army looked out the window upon their approach, she (or "her ladyship," as the *Woburn Advertiser* reported) at once realized she was out numbered and "made no demonstration." So the harvesting progressed without incident and Aurora's army was outflanked.

Soon after, in August of 1875, Aurora began a letter-writing campaign to the Woburn Selectmen. It seems she was plum out of food supplies and was requesting that they send her "the necessities of life." The town responded by sending her enough supplies to "sustain life." They also notified the City of Boston, because since Aurora Phelps was at one time a legal resident there they believed Boston should bear some responsibility for her support. Their hope was that it would result in Aurora Village being moved to another "burg" and get Woburn off the hook.

In the meantime, John Nelson was busy working on another tactic. He sold the property on which Aurora Village sat to Charles Wingate in the hopes that Wingate would have her evicted and she would "pack up and leave, willing or unwilling."

But that didn't deter Aurora Phelps. She fought back by starting another letter-writing campaign, this time forwarding copies to the local newspapers explaining her side of the story. One letter, written on November 12, 1875, told of the unfair treatment she had received from John Nelson. She said that she had sold him some lime, cement and bricks and he never paid her for them. Instead, he came to her house, claiming that her stove belonged to him and he wanted it back. When she refused, he threatened to return and take it by "force."

If Phelps thought this letter would touch the hearts of the men ruling Woburn, she was sadly mistaken. Instead, winter came in with a vengeance and Aurora's health continued to deteriorate. So much so that in January of 1876, she succumbed and passed on to her great reward.

The first announcement of her death appeared in the *Boston Daily Advertiser* on January 6, 1876. The obituary was scant on detail but it did expound on her lack of wisdom, and concluded that in spite of her hard work and determination, "Her shadowy dreams never came to fulfillment and she learned by sore experience that there were trials in life greater even than death."

The *Woburn Advertiser* provided much more detail as to how she came to her end. It revealed that Phelps had been ill for some time and had been confined to her bed for at least six months. It described her passing as peaceful and without pain in a rickety bed with ragged bedding in a place that was more like a barn for animals than some place for humans to live—"cheerless indeed."

She died of what was described by Woburn's Dr. Gray as "Bright's disease of the kidneys." In that lengthy obituary, the *Woburn Advertiser* spent a lot of ink trying to justify their change of heart toward Aurora Phelps, and concluded that although her heart was in the right place she didn't have the necessary diplomatic skills to carry out her mission. And it was with that gross understatement that the "GRAND UPRISING OF THE AMAZONS" ended and a noble effort to empower women suffered yet another setback.

WOBURN'S WITCHES

It must have come as quite a shock when Woburn Constable Ephraim Bock pounded on Ann Sears's door that cool, sunny day in May of 1692 and dragged her off to Salem Village with nothing but the clothes on her back. Up to that moment, it had been just another day in the life of Mrs. Ann Sears, third wife of John Sears, a man well-established in Woburn society since 1640, when he subscribed to Woburn Town Orders and was admitted to the church the following March of 1641.

Ann had already been widowed once, when her husband, Jacob Farrar of Lancaster, died in Woburn on August 14, 1677, while visiting with his brother, John Farrar. And since Ann was nearing her golden years, she jumped at the chance to marry John Sears in November of 1680, a marriage most likely arranged by her brother-in-law.

Sears was a good catch. In spite of the fact he was nearly fifteen years her senior, as a former town selectman, he had some status, and with no heirs, she stood to inherit all his property. Things were looking good until that day in May when she found herself accused of witchcraft.

I have not been able to uncover the connection between the three Woburn women accused of witchcraft and the principal accusers in Salem, but the warrant for Ann's arrest says that Ann Sears was accused of "high Suspicion of Sundry acts of Witchcraft done by [her] upon the Bodys of Ann Putnam, Marcy Lewis, Mary Walcot, etc. [the principal accusers] of Salem Village whereby much hurt and wrong was done unto them therefore craves justice." How Ann accomplished such a dastardly act over such a long distance is a mystery, but it may be that someone else had their eye on John Sears's property and felt that with Ann out of the way, they would be in line to inherit it.

In any case, it was that accusation that caused Ann to be brought to the house of Lieutenant Nathaniel Ingersall in Salem Village for examination relating to the charges aforementioned. Pursuant to her humiliating examination, she was removed to Cambridge Goal and held on suspicion of witchcraft until December 3, 1692. That was the day she was brought before the Middlesex Court in Cambridge and released on her own personal recognizance, promising to make an appearance when the court so ordered. But as we all know, cooler heads prevailed soon after and the case against Ann Sears was dropped.

The other two Woburn women who were accused were hardly innocents. But I doubt their crimes can be connected to witchcraft by any stretch of the imagination. It's more likely the cause can be laid to lack of character.

That same day in May that Constable Bock knocked on Ann Sears's door, he came knocking for Bethia Carter Sr. and her daughter, Bethia Jr. But a mere six days later, on May 14, 1692, another warrant was issued for Bethia Jr., and it became necessary for Constable Bock to make two trips to the Carter home.

In the end, though, both Bethia Sr. and Bethia Jr. were brought before the court at Salem Village for examination, then to Cambridge Goal for internment. This time, what was different about Constable Bock's visit was that he was no stranger to the Carter home. Only seven years previous, he had come knocking for Bethia Sr.'s husband, Joseph.

Joseph and Bethia had been married for fifteen years in 1685 and had six of their seven children at the time. But Joseph was anything but faithful. In fact, rumors had been circulating that year that it was Joseph who was the father of Joanna Negro's child. Joanna was the servant of Francis Wyman when she gave birth to a light-complexioned child that she had claimed belonged to Sampson Negro, Joseph's father's servant. But once the child was born and everyone noted its fair skin and straight brown hair, questions began to arise. Finally, when Joanna and Joseph were brought into court to settle paternity of the child, Joanna told her story.

As reported in Roger Thompson's *Sex in Middlesex*, Joanna testified that Joseph Carter "got her with child in the dyke near the well" at a time when most able-bodied men had left for Boston for their regular military training, "and his wife was gone to Reading." Once the deed was done, Joseph "bid her lay the blame to Samson, Captain Carter's Negro man" and "two month after" that "he brought Savin [an abortionist] to her and said she might take that [a potion] and it would kill the child." He "further bid her to smother the child as soon as it was born" and "if she laid it [the blame] to him he would set the devil to work upon her and she should never have a quiet life again."

Upon hearing Joanna's complaint and Joseph Carter's denial, Magistrate William Johnson claimed that since Joanna had named Sampson and then changed her mind, he found no wrongdoing on Carter's part and sentenced Joanna to jail. Joanna had named Sampson early on but recanted shortly after, explaining to Magistrate Johnson that she feared for her safety as it was Joseph's wife Bethia who was to be her midwife. But there was no way Joanna would win, and she was sentenced; since Joseph denied that he was the father, the court took his side and believed him and sentenced Joanna instead. It is reported that Joseph died a short time after this incident, but not before having another child by Bethia, Faith, on April 28, 1688.

But the Carters were to pay for their sins in other ways. In 1692, both Joseph's wife and daughter, Bethia Sr and Bethia Jr, were charged with witchcraft and "imprisoned in Woburn." His son John was later admonished by Woburn selectmen for "misspending his time" in 1699 at age thirteen.

MISSING IN ACTION AS OF MAY 8, 1864

Although Corporal George F. Pollard is listed on the Civil War rolls as having been killed at the Battle of Laurel Hill on May 8, 1864, there is no clear record of his death. In fact, reports of his death may only be an educated guess on the part of those compiling the list of Woburn men killed in the Civil War. The fact is that George Pollard's actual whereabouts were never officially confirmed. He went missing on May 8, 1864, and in spite of tireless searching on the part of two very distinguished Woburn citizens, his family had not received confirmation of his death as of June 19, 1864.

When I first began reading George Pollard's Civil War letters, I immediately felt a connection. He was a man of compassion and not prone to exaggerate. In fact, he made a point of constantly reminding everyone that he was not a hero and was, in fact, in some instances, not cut out to be a soldier. But he did his duty faithfully. As he wrote in his last letter home to his family in Woburn:

> We are engaged in a great Cause. It was one motive that prompted us all to leave all which was dear to us and come here, and now it seems to me we ought to work together hand in hand for the object for which we enlisted…I look through the cloud that hangs over us and see the times when I shall be with you when this war shall be closed and this country shall be Free, happy and united.

But George Pollard never did return home. Instead, he vanished on a bloody battlefield, never to be seen or heard from again and amid

Company G, Fifth Regiment, at camp on July 23, 1885. *Courtesy of John McElhiney.*

conflicting reports being sent home as to his destiny. On May 17, 1864, the first reports were sent of Woburn men "killed, wounded or missing" in that bloody fourteen-day Virginia campaign, and listed Corporal George F. Pollard among five members of Company K, Thirty-ninth Massachusetts Regiment missing in action.

The long and deadly Virginia campaign included the Battles of Laurel Hill and the Spotsylvania Courthouse, battles listed among the bloodiest of the Civil War. But what is not always mentioned was that weather conditions were such that many men fell unconscious from sunstroke and were left for dead or to be captured by the enemy. So it was that Woburn Selectmen sent two of their most distinguished and trustworthy citizens to Washington, D.C., to learn as much as they could about the fate of our young men.

Those two honorable men were C.S. Converse, Esq., of Hart and Company express, and Nathan Wyman, Esq., Woburn's esteemed town clerk. The two arrived in Washington on May 16, 1864, and spent their time visiting hospitals and following the trails of all Woburn soldiers found listed among the dead, wounded or taken captive. They also "rendered assistance" along the way, making sure any injured man had what he needed to get well and leaving behind money for "crutches, slippers, socks," and more.

Wyman and Converse exhaustively searched hospitals in Alexandria and Fairfax, Virginia, as well as in Washington, D.C., and spent day and night searching the lists available of more than three thousand names, visiting and interviewing everyone at the Wenham Barracks and following up at many other hospitals. They finally decided that Lieutenant Wyman, Corporal George Pollard, Privates Charles Bush, Robert Corey and Silas Waite—all of Company K, Thirty-ninth Massachusetts Regiment—had most likely been captured.

Wyman was last seen on May 8, 1864, by the men of Company D, leading his troops "in advance of the line"—among those troops was George Pollard. Lending credibility to their report, George E. Fowle of Company K also reported seeing Pollard that day and described his encounter this way: "Pollard is missing. I saw him come back after we were drove back. He was about played out with the heat before we made our last charge. I think he became exhausted and was taken prisoner. I hope it so."

Pollard's family acknowledged Fowle's observation in a letter explaining to other family members that they, too, had received a letter from Fowle on May 11, 1864, claiming that brother George most likely had been taken prisoner—if he'd been killed or injured, the company would certainly have been notified and would have reported it. In fact, according to a letter to George's brother Cyrus, written by his other brother Joseph on May 16, 1864, there was little hope that George had survived that fourteen-day battle.

The Woburn Armory on Montvale Avenue and Prospect Street, 1892–1917, and used as a police station and district court.

"I am sorry to send you such news for I fear it will fall sadly on your heart and Charlie's, but this is one of the fortunes of war and I can only leave our dear soldier brother in the hand of God praying that we all may have grace and strength to bear up under all this dreadful waiting to learn of his destiny."

Finally, on June 3, 1864, Privates Curry and Waite were accounted for. Curry had been taken prisoner at Spotsylvania Courthouse on May 8, was paroled and had rejoined his unit on the front lines. Wait, on the other hand, was reported to have been killed on that day and his body left undiscovered. But like Pollard, Private Bush and Lieutenant Wyman were still reported missing, although everyone still held out hope that all three would be found, one way or another. Shortly after this, Lieutenant Wyman's whereabouts were reported, leaving Bush and Pollard still unaccounted for.

In a letter written by George's sister Emily to her brother Charlie on June 19, 1864, Emily wrote:

> We have waited all this time and have heard nothing definite in regard to poor George. His fate still remains a mystery to us. Gilcrist feels sure he is a prisoner. How much longer have we got to wait before we hear anything from him we can't tell. Perhaps it may be months but it seems sometimes as though we should give up by that time.

And give up they did. When the memorial to the Civil War dead was finally engraved with the names of the men killed in battle, Corporal George F. Pollard's name was among them. That designation was made based on the reports compiled by Town Clerk Nathan Wyman, who himself remained uncertain of Pollard's fate.

(The letters cited are part of the "George Pollard Papers 1862–1864," in the Pearce Civil War Collection at Navarro College in Corsicana, Texas.)

WOBURN BASEBALL HISTORY, 1860–1929

Woburn, Sept. 7th, 1860. To the Zouave Base Ball Club of Stoneham:

We the members of the Winnehassett Base Ball Club of Woburn, 14 in number, do hereby challenge any 14 of your club, to meet us in a match game, according to the rules of the New England Association of Base Ball Players, on Tuesday, Sept. 18th.

With this simple challenge, published in the *Woburn Journal* on September 15, 1860, Woburn's baseball history began. In the days when "base ball" was not yet a compound word, Woburn, like every major city on the East Coast, became obsessed with "America's favorite pastime." Woburn embraced the sport of baseball with a passion that has shaped this city's love of sports on through to today. Baseball became the sporting and social life of Woburn residents for the next eighty years, until its young men were called away to fight in World War II.

Unfortunately, the Woburn Winnehassett Club's first foray into athletic competition was unsuccessful. They lost to Zouvae Club in ten innings—seventy-five to two. It seems that the newly formed Winnehasset Club had taken on a giant when it challenged Zouave. Zouave, according to all accounts, had thrashed most of its opponents by scores equal to or exceeding the seventy-five runs it logged against Winnehassett. High scores were not unusual in those early days of baseball. The pitcher's job was to merely put the ball in play. It was then up to the fielders to do the defensive work. One defensive play, called "plugging," involved throwing the ball at the runner and "plugging" him for an out.

Woburn's early losses didn't dampen the enthusiasm of local fans, who flocked to cheer and live vicariously through the sporting endeavors of young men who were to become the heroes of the day. If anything, it fed a competitive spirit that caused the number of city teams to flourish. Throughout the 1860s, teams of all sorts drew spectators to fields all over Woburn that became the stuff of dreams. In 1867, when the Union Club offered its grounds to the Mishawum Base Ball Club, they proved the theory that "If you build it, they will come"—spectators lined the playing field and cheered steadfastly in spite of the fact the Mishawum Club was summarily tromped, sixty-four to thirty-two.

In July of 1867, the *Woburn Journal* offered a room over their newspaper office where members of the Mishawum Club could meet for business as well as "social intercourse." City leagues multiplied and the Mishawum Club of Woburn Center was no longer the only game in town. The Websters of North Woburn (1868, and who later changed their name to Fearless), Essex of Woburn Center (1871), Shamrocks (1872), Rag Rock Rockets (1873), Picked Nine of Water Street (1873), Royals (1873), Emmets of East Woburn (1875) and Eagles of West Woburn (1875) were among some of the more notable early teams that actually began winning more games than they lost, forever earning the loyalty of their fans.

By 1876, the Saturday afternoon baseball game was a staple, and Woburn teams were beginning to win with regularity. Woburn's victory over a strong Arlington team brought about this remark from a *Woburn Journal* reporter: "The Woburn Base Ball players went to Arlington last Monday, and strange to say came home with the emblem of victory." Finally, faithful fans had something to cheer about.

By 1889, nearly every organization and business in Woburn sponsored a team and recruited players from all over New England. The *Woburn Journal* announced in May of 1889 that "the St. Charles have secured Twohey, formerly of the Mathew's of Lowell, as a regular pitcher." They planned to play Twohey in the annual Fourth of July game, a maneuver that got them in some difficulty when they tried to arrange a game with the Woburns.

"There was talk around now to the effect that the Woburns will object to Twohey pitching for the St. Charles team against them July 4, on the grounds that he is not a Woburn man," the *Journal* reported. But since Twohey was not hired specifically to play against the Woburns, it was considered a nonissue, but "St. Charles say they would not put him in to pitch if he is objected to." In fact, later in July, two outstanding St. Charles players, Larkin and Mathews, "played with the Woburns, not however

The Woburn High School baseball team (date unknown). *Courtesy of the Woburn Public Library Archives, Woburn, Massachusetts.*

in their regular positions. Mathews covered second for them and Larkin played in the field."

The St. Charles teams of the late 1880s and 1890s were so loaded with talent that it made no difference to them if Twohey pitched or Larkin and Mathews played for the opposing team. They continued to pile on a winning record and capped each year by taking home purses of twenty-five dollars and fifty dollars offered to the winner of the Labor Day spectaculars against the Woburns. St. Charles won easily in that first game of 1889, ten to zero. The St. Charles Reserves, as they were more formerly known, continued their winning streak until the 1920s.

In spite of a stellar assembly of talented players in the early 1900s, which included the famed "Doherty twins," a *Woburn Journal* report in 1907 claimed that "interest in Base Ball is on the wane" and lamented "the old days…when every other boy 6–20 carried a bat around." The problem was people flocked to the games, but balked at paying the admission fees that supported the teams. But baseball has always survived those old laments. According to Ruth Boyden, a baseball fan whose ninety-nine years can attest to having seen many a baseball game at Library Field, there was never any doubt that baseball would thrive. She remembers a Woburn High game about 1916 when a fire erupted in a building behind the stands. As firefighters fought the raging inferno and rescued the occupants from the building, Ruth remembers that no one left their seats and only intermittently glanced over their shoulder to see how things were going.

Two to four thousand fans flocked to Library Park to watch teams like the ones Woburn High and the city leagues produced in 1914. Players like Hal "Kiko" Weafer, who was referred to as the "original nutcracker and necksnapper"; Henry "Doc" McMahon, whose pitching was key to his all-Woburn team's success; Connie O'Doherty, whose left-handed batting was considered a handicap but went on to play for Harvard and the Boston Braves; "Rabbit" Martin, whose speed at fielding and running the bases earned him his nickname; and Steve Colucci, whose eighteen continuous innings of stellar pitching for Woburn High is a record which still holds, ensured that interest was kept high.

But there were other distractions at the ball field. The *Woburn Daily Times* of August 15, 1914, reported that "betting was as frequent as bum reports of the European war," and there was "Woburn money galore." It's no wonder that free flow of money finally corrupted the game with the Black Sox Scandal of 1919, when players fixed the World Series to collect big payoffs.

In May of 1920, an Industrial League was formed and teams like Merrimac Chemical, Beggs & Cobbs, Van Tarrell Tanning, James Robertson and Woburn Machine dominated the field. Many of the stars of these teams and Woburn High baseball went on to play pro or college ball. Among them were several sets of brothers like Ken and Ronnie Weafer, Bob and Charlie Walsh and the dynamic trio of Bart, Marty and Festy McDonough. Ken Weafer signed with the Chicago Cubs and brother Ronnie with the Philadelphia Athletics. Bob Walsh played at Dartmouth and his brother Charlie "Tweet" signed with the Chicago Cubs. But the year "Tweet" signed, the Cubs also signed Roger Hornsby, who overshadowed "Tweet" and went on to the Hall of Fame. Bart McDonough became an all-star catcher for Holy Cross, Marty plied his trade at Colgate and Festy played for University of Vermont and ended up in the Northern Pro League.

But one cannot sum up those years between 1860 and 1929 without mentioning the Golden Sox of Woburn, a group of "local young ladies" who in 1912 tied the Stoneham girls team with only eight players on the field. The *Woburn Times* of August 26, 1912, reported that "Miss Katherine Finnerty...struck out 17 opposing batters, allowed only three hits and gave only two passes" while Miss Hazel Connors and Miss Marion Kerrigan had two runs to their credit. Miss Katherine Griffin let nothing by her at first base, and Miss Beatrice Meehan, "the diminutive second baseman...displayed cleverness in the field and at bat."

There were many, many more stars of Woburn's golden years of baseball that deserve mention and I hope my meager efforts to record some of their stories get into the archives before they are lost forever.

About the Author

Marie Coady is a columnist and freelance writer. Her column appears in *Daily Times Chronicle*, in Woburn, Massachusetts, which serves ten communities. Before joining the *Times*, she was a columnist for the *Woburn Advocate* and the *Burlington Union*, weekly newspapers among the 130 belonging to Community Newspapers. As a freelance writer, she has also been published in hundreds of mainstream newspapers, magazines and children's magazines, and she has received awards for "Excellence in Column Writing" and "Editor's Choice Awards."

Visit us at
www.historypress.net